Vicki Lansky

TOILET TRAINING

A Practical Guide to Daytime

and Nighttime Training

BOOK PEDDLERS
Minnetonka, MN
distributed to the book trade by PGW

Thanks to Editors:
Toni Burbank, Maria Mack, Kathryn Ring, Sandra Whelan,
Jeane-Marie Sohlden, Kate Moore, Carol Lowry and Abby Herstein.

Consultants:
Karen Olness, M.D., Minneapolis Children's Health Center
Judy Owens-Stively, M.D., Minneapolis Children's Health Center
Peggy Osterholm, R.N., P.N.P., Wayzata Children's Clinic
Rebecca Kajander, R.N., P.N.P., Wayzata Children's Clinic
Burton White, Ph.D., Center for Parent Education, Newton, MA
Joan Reivich, Booth Maternity Center, Philadelphia, PA
Meg Zweiback, R.N., P.N.P, M.P.H., Oakland, CA
Daniel P. Kohen, M.D., Minneapolis Children's Health Center

Special thanks to the parents who shared their words and feelings. Their quotes are reprinted with permission from Vicki Lansky's *Practical Parenting™ Newsletter* and respondents to Vicki Lansky's Practical Parenting column in *Sesame Street Magazine Parents' Guide*.

Illustrator: Jack Lindstorm

THE FAR SIDE © 1986 UNIVERSAL PRESS SYNDICATE. Reprinted with permission. All rights reserved.
Cover photo copyright © 1984 by Bill Cadge. Used with permission. All rights reserved.

ISBN: 0-916773-64-7 *(paperback packaged with KoKo Bear's New Potty book)*
ISBN: 0-916773-65-5 *(library hardcover edition without KoKo book)*

Publisher's Cataloging-in-Publication
(Provided by Quality Books, Inc.)

Lansky, Vicki.
    Toilet training : a practical guide to daytime and
nighttime training : with, KoKo Bear's new potty : a
read together book / Vicki Lansky. --1st ed.
        p.cm
        Includes index.
        ISBN 0-916773-65-5 (hc)
        ISBN 0-916773-64-7 (pb)

        1. Toilet training.   I. Lansky, Vicki. KoKo Bear's
new potty. II. Title.

HQ770.5.L36 2002   649'.62
                                     QBI02-701636

For information contact:
BOOK PEDDLERS
15245 Minnetonka Blvd • Minnetonka, MN 55345
www.bookpeddlers.com • www.practicalparenting.com
952-912-0036 • fax: 952-912-0105

PRINTED IN CHINA

02 03 04 05 06 07 08 9 8 7 6 5 4 3 2 1

CONTENTS

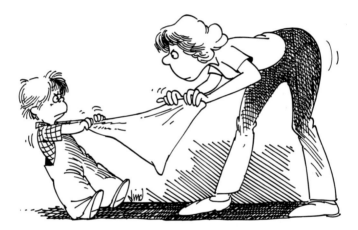

Introduction

Why Is Toilet Training Such a Big Deal?

🌷

A number of things can contribute to a parent's strong need to get a child toilet trained, *right now.* Some are pressures from your peers, fear that you're failing as a parent by tolerating a child in diapers, the enrollment of your child in preschool, and, not least, the strains and stresses of what's known as "diaper drag."

First, assume that any neighbor or relative who claims victory in toilet training her child before yours is lying (well, maybe exaggerating), fantasizing, or redefining the term. I never considered my children really trained until they could get in and out of the bathroom, get their clothes off and back on, clean their bottoms properly, and wash their hands—all without any help from me. But for now, we'll work with that more limited but still important definition that simply has the child saying, "Get me to the potty" in time.

Second, plan not to take it personally. Your child's readiness for toilet training is no indication of his or her IQ, your level of parenting ability, or your parents' attempts to raise you properly. *(Despite what your mother-in-law might imply about your 3-year-old still being in diapers, doesn't mean she did a better job than you're doing.)*

Third, be assured that it *will* happen. When your child is truly ready, physically and emotionally, toilet training will happen rapidly. And be assured that while it's going on, toilet training is very, very important, but when it's accomplished, you'll wonder why it seemed like such a big concern!

Fourth, remember that you are not alone. When your child regresses for the third time, meditate on the fact that, simultaneously, several million other mothers and fathers are earning their toilet-training merit badges, too.

One controversy on this subject is the language used to describe this process. It's called "toilet learning," "potty training," "toilet teaching," and "toileting." Yes, *learning* may be more accurate than *training*, at least according to today's wisdom, but I've never had anyone ask me if my child was toilet learned. So please bear with my preference for toilet training, and don't search for deeper meanings.

Remember that there are three things you can never make your child do —
eat, sleep, or go to the bathroom.

Chapter 1

When Is My Child Ready to Be Toilet Trained?

❦

The days of hand-hemmed, hand-washed, line-dried diapers are gone—thank goodness. So that should signal an era of more relaxed, less anxious parents, right?

Wrong!

The prospect of toilet training today evokes as much concern as it ever did. The pressures of friends and relatives—even doctors—as well as practical considerations have pushed many parents into premature toilet-training attempts that eventually ended in failure and frustration.

It is true that current wisdom has made many parents less intense about having a child trained before the age of two. Early training is no longer the norm, but once a parent decides that the time has come, relaxation seems to go out the window.

The simple fact is that your child must be physically and emotionally mature enough to understand and to control what is happening in the process. If you begin to toilet train a child before this point, the odds are that it simply won't work. A child who is "trained" before age two usually has a toilet trained parent—one who is trained to catch the child!

Physical maturation first becomes possible with voluntary control over the sphincter muscles—which means being able to open and close very specific internal muscles. While this is possible by about one and a half years, this voluntary control only truly begins when a child can distinguish the sensations that precede a bowel movement or urination. This, in turn, depends on a certain amount of maturity of the central nervous system, over which no one has control.

> **You don't toilet train children—you wait for their bodies to mature (a fact God has already worked out). I made a game of it, with a timer set for 15 minutes after drinking a liquid. My son loved it!**
>
> *Linda Hurstell, Vicksburg, MS*

Emotional readiness is also crucial. A child's sense of self starts to emerge around the age of two. For the first time, the child realizes that he or she can affect the world and his or her own life. Unfortunately, one of the first manifestations of this new found power occurs during the "terrible twos" stage when a child seems interested only in affecting his or her world negatively! It's not all bad, though.

One of the positive results of this emerging assertiveness is a desire to grow up. And one of the best examples of grown-up behavior a child can relate to is being toilet trained. Once your child arrives at this point, he or she is more likely to cooperate with your toilet training efforts because he or she wants to. Body mastery is more self-rewarding than a desire to please.

The *average* child cannot be successfully toilet trained before the age of about 28 months. While girls are often trained by two, boys may not be trained before three or later.

4

A report in the Journal of Ambulatory Pediatrics (2001) showed that the average age of completing toilet training—35 months for girls and 39 months for boys—are the oldest ages yet reported and in line with the trend of the increasing age for toilet training.

But of course the exception to prove this rule will inevitably be your neighbor's child, a child in your child's play group, or your sister-in-law's child.

Whether a child is placed on a potty seat at six weeks, six months, or 16 months, most children will not be reliable until after the age of two.

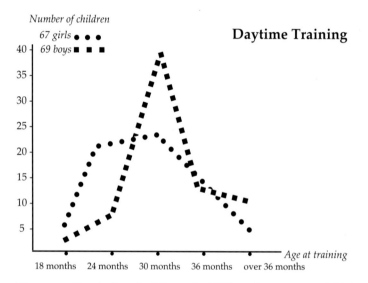

These results of a Practical Parenting™ Newsletter survey *(1984)* are similar to a 2001 study by the Medical College of Wisconsin conducted by Timothy R. Schumm, M.D.

And no two children, even siblings who have been treated in exactly the same way, will be ready at the same age. There is a right time to begin this process, but it varies from child to child.

Any time before the age of four is normal, despite what Grandma—or anyone else—says. 98% of kids are trained by age four.

You might wish to consider the advantages and disadvantages of early toilet training before making a decision to try it. By early, I mean from age one to age two.

Just as we were finished toilet training our son, our next child (a girl) started wanting to use the toilet. She would watch her brother sit on the toilet and cry to take her diaper off. I fought her for three weeks, refusing to potty train two at once. But finally I thought if she was that insistent, she was ready. I put her in training pants, and three weeks later (at 18 months) she was completely trained.
Charlotte Martin, Bartlesville, OK

Advantages of Early Toilet Training

The advantages of early toilet training are obvious. In fact, they're the same as the advantages for toilet training in general, you just get to enjoy them sooner. Parents are anxious to have their children trained for a variety of reasons. Caring for an untrained child takes more planning and a lot of equipment. Travel and baby-sitting are more cumbersome. Wet diapers can cause diaper rash. *(One mother told me her daughter trained herself in one day to escape a particularly painful case of diaper rash.)*

On the average, dealing with diapers consumes approximately ten hours a week for most parents. A year's worth of disposable diapers is costly, as is a diaper service. Cloth diapers that you launder yourself are not as cheap as they would seem, when you consider the cost of detergent, electricity, and wear and tear on the laundry equipment, not to mention Mom and Dad. Some nursery schools won't take children in diapers, or they may charge more for the inconvenience. All in all, life is a lot more pleasant and less complicated when diapers become a thing of the past. The attitude of most parents is "the sooner the better."

Disadvantages of Trying to Toilet Train Too Early

However nice it is to finally have a toilet-trained child, the process shouldn't *(and usually can't)* be rushed. Consider these disadvantages which are a high price to pay for a lowered cost of diapers:

- Trying to toilet train a child who isn't ready can prove to be futile, a waste of time and lots of unresolved anger.

- A child who is forced to try to comply may experience an extreme sense of failure. And so may the parents!

- Premature toilet training may create a war of wills in which no one wins. A child may actually hold back bowel movements, creating serious constipation problems in an attempt to control the parent.

- The stresses of futile attempts at training may cause a parent to use inappropriate regimentation or force. Studies show that one of the principal causes of child abuse is parental frustration over a child's unsuccessful toilet training.

- A child's anxiety about toilet training may lead to bed-wetting into adulthood. (A study of 18-year-old British army inductees provided a classic example of this. Fifteen percent were still bed-wetters after having been toilet trained before the age of one.)

We know that early rigid and coercive tactics are not worth the success they might achieve. In fact, rigid and coercive tactics

7

used later in the training process can ALSO create more problems than they solve!

While most professionals today advocate later-is-just-fine, Katie Van Pelt in her book, *Potty Training Your Baby* (1996), believes you should begin training before your child's first birthday. Another book promoting early training is *Infant Potty Training* by Laurie Boucke *(White-Boucke Publishing, 2000).*

I have been at odds with my four-year-old for more than two years. We seem to backslide a lot (sort of like two steps forward, one step back). I think I put too much pressure on him in the beginning. We are trying to be more laid back with our younger child.

Becky Wilkins, Lubbock, TX

As one who did not get trained until age four and a half myself, I would not suggest the issue first. Once either of ours decided he or she wanted to use the potty and wear panties, that was the key.

Jodi Junge, Huntingdon Valley, PA

What Are the Basics?

You'll probably think about toilet training long before you get into it. One thing you'll want to do is settle any major differences of opinion between you and your spouse (or anyone else who will be involved) about methods and ways of handling things. Some compromise may be called for. Basic consistency is very important. There should be total agreement that there's no place for punishment in any phase of toilet training.

General Signs of Readiness

From the time your child is about two (though it may be nearer three for some), you should watch for signs of readiness for training. If certain signs are clearly present, and the child is basically past the negative "no-to-every-request" stage, he or she is probably ready.

You'll know your child is ready when he or she:

- Is aware of the "need to go," and shows it by facial expression or by telling you.

- Can express and understand one-word statements, including such words as "wet," "dry," "potty," and "go."

- Demonstrates imitative behavior.

- Can sit quietly for 4 minutes or more.

- Dislikes wet or soiled diapers. *(Don't confuse this with your level of discomfort or inconvenience.)*

- Is anxious to please you.

- Is able to stay dry for at least two hours or wakes up dry after a nap.

- Is able to pull elastic waist pants up and down.

- Has a sense of social "appropriateness" *(wet pants can be an embarrassment).*

- Tells you he or she is "about" to go. *(Praise such statements to set the stage for a child who wishes to please you by learning to use the toilet or potty.)*

- Asks to use the potty chair or adult toilet!

Check Fluid Intake

If your child shows all the signs of readiness except the ability to stay dry for at least two hours, check fluid intake. Any child who is drinking milk, water, or fruit juices continuously cannot stay dry for long. Also, check with your doctor about the possibility of a milk allergy or lactose intolerance *(the inability to digest milk properly)* which can result in cramps, loose stools and the inability to hold a bowel movement for more than a moment.

Some Preparatory Steps

There is much to be said for setting the stage well before you begin toilet training. Few children train themselves. They need to know what's expected of them. They need and deserve your help and guidance. A child who has become familiar with bathroom procedures and equipment is more likely to become trained quickly and easily than one who has not.

- Take your child into the bathroom with you. It's especially helpful if fathers and brothers set the example for boys, and mothers and sisters set the example for girls. Siblings are often pleased to act as role models. If your privacy is important to you, don't forget that there are neighborhood children who would probably be delighted to demonstrate. Day-care today often lets children "learn" from their peers and often speeds up their learning curve.

- Try to help your child recognize the sensations of "being wet," "wetting now," and "about to be wet." Encourage your child to talk about these sensations—especially "about to be . . ." sensations—without pressuring your child to be toilet trained. Comment on signs you notice, such as the child's pausing in play or walking if he or she is uncomfortable after elimination. Use statements such as, *"You are having a BM,"* rather than asking the general question, *"What are you doing?"* Asking your child to let you know when the diaper is wet or messy is another way of increasing awareness.

- Let your child go nude in appropriate settings to help the child "see" what he or she is doing, and to help make the mental connection between the words and what they refer to.

- Changing a diaper in the bathroom will also associate the process with the place. Children over age two should be off the changing table for this reason.

- Although much ado has been made about using the proper terminology for body parts and functions, you should use the words that come most easily to you and your child. "Peeing," for example, may be more effective than the term "urinating" if the latter is a forced term. DO use specific terms, though; "going to the bathroom" is too vague. Try not to use words that will make your child think of his or her bodily functions as being dirty or disgusting (for example, "dirty," "stinky," "yucky," etc.).

- Help your child learn the meaning of the terms "before" and "after" by using them yourself in other contexts such as, *"We'll wash the dishes* after *dinner."*

- Talk about the advantages of being trained: no more diaper rash, no more interruptions for diaper changing, and the pleasure of being clean and dry. Discuss training as an important stage of growing up and being "grown up."

- Let your child practice lowering and raising training diapers or pants sometimes, or putting them on and taking them off.

- Have a potty chair handy on which the child may sit on *(even with clothes on)* while you are in the bathroom yourself, but only if he or she wants to. The intent is not to get results, but to provide familiarity with the equipment. Let the child flush the toilet for you, to help him or her get used to the noise it makes and avoid possible fear later on.

- Begin reading potty books to your child. (See page 55.)

Also watch for body signals that children give when they have the urge to go.

- Becoming red in the face.

- "Dancing" on tiptoes.

- Holds legs together.

- Pulling at clothes.

- Hands holding genital area.

You can put words to their actions and point out these signals and suggest using the bathroom. Eventually children tune into these signals themselves.

I don't think there's any one way to toilet train children. They can be tempted, coaxed, yelled at or put on the potty every hour, but they won't really be trained until they decide they're ready.

Marlene Gwiazdon, Osceola, WI

Nothing I try has worked. My three-year-old understands everything about potty training, but tells me, "I'm not ready, Mommy." So I try not to say anything. If he's not ready, he's not ready.

Kyle Lutz, Mill Valley, CA

Chapter 2

Should I Choose a Potty Chair, an Adapter or Use the Toilet Seat?

Some experts claim that we complicate the toilet training process when we require children to learn on several different kinds of equipment in succession. We start them on the potty chair, then move them to the adapter seat, and finally, we move them to the adult toilet—making three tasks for them to learn.

There is much to be said for using one, two, or all three of these methods. I suspect that the choice really isn't all that significant. Your choice will depend on your child's size, age, and preference; your preference (*which I think counts for a lot*); and the size and number of your bathrooms. Whatever method you settle on will probably work just fine for you and your child.

Potty Chairs

Proponents of the potty chair say it allows a child to be more independent, since a parent doesn't need to lift the child to the toilet. It also allows a child to place his or her feet squarely on the floor when bearing down to eliminate, and the child can also use the support of the chair arms. Because a potty chair is obviously the child's own, he or she will take pride in possessing it.

I know many parents like the flexibility of the potty chair, moving it to various rooms in the house to suit their convenience, and using it for travel as well. (Others claim that a potty chair should remain in the bathroom, so its purpose becomes solely associated with the bathroom.)

If you have a potty chair in the bathroom, you and your child can go to the toilet at the same time.

One disadvantage is that a boy will not be able to urinate standing up—it will be too difficult to aim, and there will be too much splashing. Another consideration is that it needs to be cleaned out by you or your child. In the beginning, cleaning out the pot will be fun. With experience, it loses its appeal for a child—and probably for you too.

If the potty chair appeals to you, you should get one before you start training so it becomes a familiar piece of equipment to your child. In fact, you may even let your child shop for the chair with you. You can narrow the choice down to two or three styles, and let your child choose from among those. This can make the child all the more anxious to try it out.

Personalizing a potty chair or adapter will also make it more unique and interesting. You can do this by adding a few stickers or decals of your child's choosing. Or use press-type letters and spell out your child's name.

Let your child know that it's okay—for now—to sit on the potty with clothes on to get used to it, but when he or she is ready, it will be used as *"Mommy and Daddy use the toilet."* Avoid using the potty chair at other times so as not to confuse the issue.

Choosing a Potty Chair

If you opt for a potty chair, you will probably choose a miniature version of an adult toilet, a molded one-piece style that a child straddles or a plastic molded stool-type chair. Many potty chairs today convert to adult toilet seat adapters as well.

- Before purchasing a potty chair, check to see how the pot is removed. If the pot is hard to get out or it has to be tipped, don't buy it.

- If you want a urine deflector, look for a removable one made of flexible plastic. Potties with deflectors seem to be easier to find than those without them. If your child is hurt by one when trying to seat himself, he may refuse to use the seat.

- Buy a floor model that won't slide around and is stable.

- Consider buying more than one potty chair, especially if you have more than one bathroom or a two story house. The extra one can always be used for car travel or left at grandma's.

- Be aware that if you get a potty chair with a tray, lifting it up will be one more step your child will have to master.

- Look into the possibility of buying an adult camping portable potty for a child who is unusually large.

Cleanup Responsibility

- Make cleaning the potty chair chamber easier by keeping an inch or so of water in the bottom of the pot.

- Or place a few sheets of toilet paper on the bottom for a quicker clean-up of bowel movements.

- Or cover the clean removable bowl with clear cling wrap and then just lift out the deposited contents now contained in the wrap.

- NEVER put any bleach in the bottom of a clean chamber pot. Urine contains ammonia and if a child urinates into the bleach it will cause a chemical reaction producing toxic fumes. Using bleach to disinfect the pot in the cleaning-up process, however, will not be problematic.

- Consider having your child be responsible for cleanup. Not every parent is comfortable with this, nor will every child adapt to it. Keep in mind that it's not really developmentally appropriate for a very young child.

- Fascination with feces is not unique to your toddler. To prevent a child from playing with it, take the potty chamber out of reach after use. You may need to wait a bit before flushing it if your child is insistent. This stage usually does not last too long. *Whew!*

Potty training is a lot like a first kiss. You can't do much about it—it just happens. In my daughter's case, potty training occurred over a weekend. The key, found out by accident, was that she didn't want to be taken to her potty and prompted (*how silly of me to think that would work!*) but rather, characteristically, wanted to do it herself. Once we got that straight, all I had to do was praise the results.
Kathe Grooms, St. Paul, MN

Sit on It!

There are many potty chairs available to you. Most stores tend to carry one to three styles. Many styles convert from floor models to use as toilet seat adapters. You can always call a store first to see whose brands they carry (and the price) or surf the web checking out what is available. Several mail order catalogs also offer a variety of models.

Many of today's potty seats are made by companies that also specialize in toys. Their plastic injection molding techniques have been transferred to other juvenile products, such as potty chairs, which make them sturdy and safe items to use.

There are ones that offer music (usually moisture activated), some that are one piece molds and others that are more complex to try to stand out from the crowd.

One on-line source offering a number of different styles is www.pottytrainingsolutions.com.

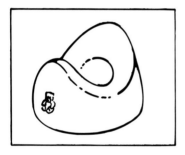
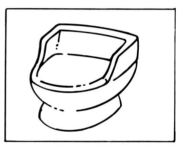

Choosing an Adult Toilet Seat Adapter

Many of today's toilet top adapters come from the multi-use floor models. But they can be purchased by themselves also. Some come as seats, others are molded padded rings, and one popular flip-up style attaches to your toilet seat and lifts up when not in use. There are some with steps attached to the adapter giving support to hands and feet. All of these offer the same help which is to reduce the opening of adult toilet seats for small size bottoms.

Potty adapters are lightweight and portable and have the additional advantage of direct flushing, so there is no extra cleanup necessary. However, adapter seats can be a nuisance for the rest of the family if there is only one bathroom and the adapter is in the way and must constantly be removed and replaced.

Many of these seats come with vinyl straps implying that a child can be left alone on the seat and needs extra safety protection. In the early stages of training, a child should not be left alone. No child should be strapped in place and then left! That is likely to feel like punishment to a child. Stay with your child. If you haven't gotten the desired results within three to five minutes, you probably aren't going to. Parents sometimes use this as a time to read to their child (potty books or otherwise) so a child can relax while sitting on the toilet.

 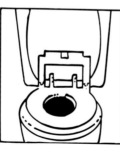 

As children take on the responsibility of using the toilet with an adapter, they will be on and off by themselves in no time, and the strap will be unnecessary, though a footstool will be needed.

There is an inflatable potty with disposable plastic bag liners as well as a folding adapter seat that fits in your purse. These are good for use when traveling (see *Traveling During Training*, page 71) or shopping. The fold-up style works well for that extra bathroom at home when you don't wish to purchase an additional potty seat. It is also a sanitary solution when using public toilets.

These are available from several mail order catalogs as well as from Practical Parenting *(800-255-3379)*. See page 104.

Footstools for Solid Footing

You should have a sturdy footstool available to help your child get up on the adult toilet adapter seat. This is also helpful for the child who has learned to use the adult toilet without an adapter seat. A stool can be of value for a small boy who isn't tall enough to urinate over the edge of the toilet bowl. It also gives a child having a bowel movement a solid footing to push and bear down on.

Footstools can be used afterward to reach the sink and wash hands—an important habit that needs to be established early. Quality wooden footstools are expensive but are usually a good, long term investment. You will find many uses for them over the years in various parts of your home. Many multi-use potty chairs we have mentioned, turn into footstools. But any footstool will do. A good footstool is important to have—probably more so—than even a potty chair.

As far as toilet training my daughter, I've decided to leave it up to her (future) husband!

Lynn Souter, Onalaska, WI

I know lots of people have used stickers as rewards during toilet training. We let my son choose a sticker and put it on the inside of the lid of the toilet. It worked like a charm, and looks cute, too.

Susan Boozier, Irvine, CA

Direct Use of the Toilet

It is perfectly acceptable to have your child learn to use the toilet without any special equipment. Obviously, the longer you wait to train your child, the bigger he or she will be and the more likely to sit on an adult seat without any aid except possibly yours.

It takes some practice to sit on the toilet. It requires more balance than most adults realize. The adult toilet can seem like an abyss to a child. But certain techniques can make a child feel more secure.

- Teach a boy to urinate sitting down backward on the toilet, straddling it, and pointing his penis downward. If he is distracted while standing, he might forget to aim.

- Teach a little girl to sit sideways or backward on the big toilet. A little girl should also "sink" her bottom low enough so urine does not go through an adapter seat ring or the bowl rim. In the beginning, removing underwear and pants will lessen the chance of them getting wet.

- Hold your child securely on the seat's edge yourself.

21

T.P. Control

Learning moderation in the use of toilet paper is also part of the training process.

- Impress upon a child that four squares of toilet paper will do the job effectively! Another measuring trick is to roll the paper down until it touches the floor. Or have a child take a strip of tissue the length of his or her arm.

- Reduce the use of excessive paper by making it harder to unroll. Before putting a roll of paper in place, press against it with the palm of your hand, in effect, squishing its natural contour. Now it will not turn as readily, increasing the chance of a child only taking what is needed, not what is easily unrolled.

- For a child who treats T.P. as an object of play, keep it off its natural holder for now but within reach. Place a rubberband around the roll that will be easy for you to remove but will be an obstacle for your child.

- Or cut off a center section the same size as the horizontal dimension of a roll of toilet paper from an empty plastic pop liter bottle. Slit it up the side and trim it to fit the roll. It will act as a see-through cover to the toilet paper roll that will be easy for you to slip on and off the roll of toilet paper but virtually impossible for a child's small hands to do so. *(Also a good deterrent for pets who think T.P. is for playing!)*

- Put the roll on *backward* so the paper comes from the back. Usually a child "slaps" paper down—not up—so there's less chance of excess unrolling.

Hygiene

Wiping seems to remain a parental responsibility for quite a while, even after a child has assumed much or all of the other responsibilities associated with toilet training. It is difficult for children to do a good job of wiping. Poor cleanup can be irritating, in more ways than one.

Stressing Good Habits from the Beginning

- Teach a child, especially a girl, to wipe from front to back. (Wiping from back to front can cause infections.)

- Let your child use flushable, premoistened babywipes after bowel movements. They are easier to use and many parents claim their use cuts down dramatically on laundry. They can also be used for hand hygiene before leaving the bathroom.

- Help your child understand to keep using new pieces of paper until there is no brown stain.

- Insist that hands be washed after using the toilet, and supply pretty hand towels and liquid soap to make the task less boring.

- Attach a hand towel to a towel bar with a shower curtain or blanket clip. That keeps it accessible yet off the floor.

Chapter 3

How Do I Begin Toilet Training?

Toilet training is a learning process, not a disciplinary process, and a complicated one at that! Your child has to understand what you want, and then has to learn how to do it. In addition to understanding the bodily sensations, getting to the bathroom and getting clothes off, a child must first constrict sphincter muscles to achieve control, and then relax them to eliminate. Obviously there is a lot to learn. Gaining bowel and bladder control is a skill and fortunately children like to learn new skills.

The mastery of skills usually follows a pattern. First comes *bowel regularity* often followed by *bowel control. Daytime bladder control* usually comes next but for many children this can happen simultaneously, and finally later *(often much later)*, comes *nighttime bladder control.* 20% of toddlers 18 to 30-month-old will initially use a potty to urinate but not to move their bowels. That step occurs within the next six months for most of these kids, say researchers from the Pennsylvania School of Medicine.

Not every child will follow this pattern, of course. While girls often achieve control before boys, brothers have been known to be dry before same-age sisters. Also, it is not uncommon, especially for boys over the age of three, to have bladder control but not have bowel control. And, of course, there are children who achieve daytime and nighttime control simultaneously. With the swing toward a more relaxed approach to toilet training from the previous generation *(some say "too relaxed")*, children tend to be trained later and thus their bowel and bladder functions frequently come under their control at the same time.

With the advent of disposables that wick away wetness from the skin, children are often quite happy to continue to wear diapers. Experts, such as Dr. Brazelton, have even gone on record that age four is a perfectly acceptable age for toilet training. These are some of the factors that have made this process often occur later today than in the past.

If you do choose a passive, more laissez-faire attitude about toilet training, keep in mind that children still need to know what it is that is expected of them. You are not necessarily "pushing" your child by providing direction and expectations. Some children really are ready to be trained early, so you are not "pushing" if you are meeting no resistance. Let their resistance be your guide. Children really do love learning grown-up behavior, so don't deny them their opportunity, if it fits their readiness.

> **My son was potty trained in three days at the age of 18 months. I had a potty chair in our bathroom. The trick was he *always* mimicked his daddy. *(Daddy did have to sit down for a while, though!)***
>
> *Rose M. Arndt Kurturin, Knox, IN*

Bowel Control

At some point your child will no longer have bowel movements during the night. This becomes a daytime process for most children. The more regular your child is, the easier it will be to start bowel-control training. Children often stop playing when they are having a BM. Some even hide in a favorite spot. Others just grunt or get red in the face. Saying, *"I see you're having a BM"* helps a child identify what is occurring and associate those sensations with the process.

Constipation, as explained in greater detail on page 29, if part of your child's history, may actually delay toilet training. This is not anything to be worried about, but just one more variable you can be sensitive to.

Explain to your child that you will be taking him or her to the toilet or the potty chair and that you expect the bowel movement to go there rather than in diapers. *"This is what Mommy and Daddy do, what grown-ups do and now what you should do because you're getting so big and grown up"* is the kind of language to use. Give advance notice about when this procedure will start. Children need to hear what you expect in pleasant tones and words. They can't read your mind. Your attitude, your anticipation, your relaxed tones will also convey much of the message.

- If your child has a regular time for a bowel movement, choose that time to go to the bathroom.

- If there is no regular time, try within 30 minutes after a meal. When the stomach is full, the colon is often stimulated to empty.

- Consider putting feces into the potty container to show the child where it goes, as some parents have.

- Be prepared to sit with your child to keep him or her company. Don't insist your child sit for more than a few minutes but only as long as he or she is comfortable.

- Know that some children need to be alone to have a bowel movement. Bright bathroom lights and too much conversation may inhibit them from relaxing their sphincter muscles.

- Praise your child for every bowel movement made in the potty or toilet. Also praise a child for even sitting and trying to go.

- If your child will still be wearing disposable diapers at this point, you will be involved in getting them on and off. Masking tape can be used to refasten clean ones.

To Flush or Not to Flush?
That is the Question

It is not unusual for a child to find such satisfaction in passing a bowel movement that he or she wants to keep or to play with the feces and will resist having them flushed down the toilet. You may need to leave them in the toilet for a few minutes before flushing or do the flushing yourself after your child has left the bathroom, especially in beginning toilet training. Other children prefer to wave "bye-bye" and do their own flushing. Having control over the flushing can make it less scary for a fearful child.

While the child who views feces as modeling clay must be corrected, it is best not to refer to them as *"dirty"* or *"yucky."* A child may find it hard to forgive you or may feel demoralized by such comments. It may hurt a child to hear that this part of the body is bad or dirty and is being flushed away for that reason. Children may feel these words apply to themselves rather than to what they've "made." Explain that feces are the *"extras"* that your body doesn't need.

Belated Bowel Control

It is not uncommon for boys to achieve bladder control before—
sometimes LONG before—bowel control. Parents sometimes
feel that a child with belated bowel control is unwilling, uncoop-
erative, or just plain stubborn but that's rarely the case. Researchers in a January 1997 article studied a small group of children to
see whether kids who refused to use the potty for bowel movements had more behavior problems than toilet-trained children.
They didn't.

A reluctant-relaxer may require different approaches until
you find one that works. Using a footstool so feet can be on a solid
surface can be helpful. Consider breaking the task into small,
slow steps. Encourage a child to sit on and use the potty (or toilet)
with clothes and a disposable diaper on to begin with. After a
child is comfortable with this procedure, progress to going with
only a disposable diaper—sides ripped open. Then you can
move from sitting with a disposable diaper across the seat to just
using toilet paper across it. Other children may be able to relax
and void (just remove feces quickly with little fuss) while in a
warm bath before making the transition to the potty chair or
toilet. Or insist, that even using a diaper, a child stay in the
bathroom when having a BM and then empty the diaper into the
toilet and flush.

According to a 1997 study by Dr. Bruce Taubman at the
University of Pennsylvania School of Medicine, "stool-toileting
refusal" is common. Some 20% of children in his study refused to
use the potty for bowel movements for at least one month. 85%
of the "stool-toileting refusers" wore underpants but asked for a
diaper for a bowel movement, or waited until they were put in
one for naps or bedtime before they would eliminate. When
asked how to change this behavior, Dr. Taubman said to take
them out of underpants and put them back in diapers and ignore
the problem. They will decide for themselves when to start
pooping in the toilet.

Constipation

Constipation is often a factor in belated bowel control. A child who cries, screams, or kicks when urged to use the potty may be doing so because of the discomfort or pain experienced due to constipation. In this case, it is not stubbornness, but fear *(real or imagined)*, that is keeping the child from doing what you ask and holding back. Some even believe there can be an inherited tendency towards constipation.

Constipation is NOT diagnosed by *infrequency* of bowel movements, but by the *hardness* and *character* of the stool. Dry BMs that don't stick to the diaper can be a description of constipation. And what may be considered hard to pass by adult standards is not the same for children. Whatever makes passing stool difficult or painful for a child will inhibit a child from wishing to repeat the procedure thus compounding the problem. Avoid suppositories and enemas . They will be seen as an "assault" by the child. The first step in treating constipation—real or suspected—is to change the child's diet.

- Decrease milk products (milk, cheese, ice cream, etc.). If a doctor recommends eliminating milk products for any length of time, a calcium supplement will probably be recommended.

- Decrease or eliminate apples, bananas, rice, and gelatin. These are binders. Opt for peaches, instead.

- Chocolate is a constipating food especially when consumed in quantity. Some medications, too.

- Increase whole-grain breads, cereals, muffins, and any other bran foods. Add bran to other foods. If your child will only eat bran cereal with milk, and you're trying to cut down on milk, dilute the milk with water. Offer graham crackers rather than soda crackers. Roughage helps.

- Possibly decrease fluid intake (milk, juices, sodas) to increase a child's appetite for bulkier foods. However, remember that fluids are important if you are dealing with constipation and shouldn't be drastically reduced. Encourage your child to drink water.

- Try prunes—the old standby—and dried fruits (if you can get your child to eat them!). Prune juice can be mixed with a small amount of milk. Encourage your child to eat fruits and vegetables with skins on, seeds, and berries for the fiber value. Fruit nectars are good too.

- Mild laxatives, to use only in conjunction with your doctor, are: a spoonful of honey; a little milk of magnesia or a bit of mineral oil camouflaged in something else.

Expect to wait two weeks or so before seeing a noticeable change in bowel movements after starting a new diet. Don't resume bowel training until such a change occurs.

Very *loose* stools can also inhibit bowel control but are often a sign of other problems (infection, milk allergy, etc.) indicating that a physician should be consulted. Food allergies causing chronic diarrhea can also cause "wear and tear" making it difficult to have bowel movements. A diet change may be recommended, but it should be done in conjunction with medical advice. But first just try eliminating apple juice—and other sweet juices—especially if your child drinks a lot of them, to see if that helps firm up bowel movements.

While it is helpful to track down the cause for belated bowel performance when you can, there is still little available to parents on how to handle this situation. I can not tell you how often I've heard this issue raised and how seldom I've seen helpful advice from those who have had to deal with it. I can only guess that once past this hurdle *(one it seems most children get past on their own)*, parents no longer are interested in the topic or even tell their doctors how it happened. Perhaps this alone will reassure those coping with this stressful situation to relax and let it play out on its own.

> When I was training my daughter, she would do *all* her business in her training pants until we decided she had to rinse out her own panties.
>
> *Rowena Cook, Anniston, AL*
>
> My son learned to urinate in the toilet when he was two years and seven months. However, he did not have the patience to sit and wait for a bowel movement. When he soiled his "big boy" pants, I asked him to remove his pants, pick up the stool with toilet paper, clean the floor and his underpants. After four days of this he decided it was lots easier to sit on the toilet!
>
> *Esta Drucker Sobey, Wilbraham, MA*
>
> At age 3, my son was content to wear one diaper all day long. He was too busy to have it changed or go to the potty. One day I took away the plastic pants, so he had to have his clothing changed very frequently. He was potty trained in about 6 hours!
>
> *Mrs. L. G. Williams, Pineville, NC*

VERY Belated Bowel Control

Encopresis is the term used for lack of control of bowel movements for anyone over the age of four. It is *NOT* uncommon. In fact it is reported that 1%–2% of children over age four are known as "fecally incontinent." For unknown reasons it is more common for boys than girls. It has incorrectly been assumed that this is the result of emotional disorders (which are more often the result—*not the cause*—of it) or by lax toilet training. A child can also be born with poor muscle tone in the bowel or anal sphincter. It seems, however, the majority of cases are the result of chronic constipation as discussed before, though it can be complicated by other stresses in either toilet training or life situations. With chronic constipation, colon tissue can be stretched to the point that nerves fail to receive proper signals and the muscles no longer contract properly so that a child no longer feels the urge to go.

A child may even have no awareness of when stool pushes out into the underwear. Watery stools can also seep past harder stool, soiling pants without a child being aware of it until after the fact. Regardless of the basis of the problem, both parents and children need to know they are not alone here and no one is to blame for this problem.

Not all doctors are trained in successful therapy for this problem so look to find one that is, as this problem needs to be approached medically as well as psychologically. If your county medical association can't help you, seek out a children's hospital or university teaching hospital near you. Encopresis is treated by a gradual retraining of the bowel which includes dietary changes, supplements, and behavior modification. There is not an overnight cure for this condition.

One helpful workbook for parents and children dealing with encopresis is *Childhood Constipation and Soiling* published by Dr. Dan Kohen, Behavioral Services of Minneapolis Children's Medical Center (*612-813-6816*). And there is a children's book, *Clouds & Clocks: A Story for Children Who Soil* by M. Galvin (Magination Press, *800-374-2721*).

Daytime Bladder Control

Some parents prefer to begin toilet training in the winter or rainy months when it's hard to get out of the house, but I think it is easiest to begin toilet training in the summer if this fits your schedule. Summer clothes are light and can be removed quickly. And when accidents do occur, you'll have fewer layers of clothes to launder.

If possible, plan to devote at least three days in a row to begin bladder training and give your child your complete attention. During those days you must be able to drop everything when a child has to go.

- Tell your child that you expect to be told if there is a need to go.

- Let your child be in charge of as much of the toilet training process as possible.

- Put a child on the toilet or potty first thing in the morning, before naps, after naps, after meals, after being dry for two hours, and before bedtime. Initially a regular schedule can help with this process.

- Turn the water on and let it run for "inspiration," or sprinkle warm water over a child's genitals.

- Offer more fluids when you are actively involved in training. The more a child drinks, the more a child will need to urinate and respond to body signals.

- Use the reminder as a "before" condition: *"After you use the potty, we will . . ."*

- Praise all progress. For some, sitting more than 10 seconds may be progress. Overlook "failures." *(Can a normal body function be a "failure"?)* Avoid punishments.

- Say occasionally *"it's time to try now."*

- Set a timer to remind your child when it's time to go potty rather than doing all the reminding yourself."

- Consolidate success by maintaining the same routine for several weeks.

- Keep your child company—unstrapped—on a potty chair or adapter. Use the time for reading. Books about potties are appropriate selections to keep in the bathroom.

    Keep in mind that even children who have mastered the bathroom procedure may wet their pants during the day for several weeks or months.
    If you have followed all reasonable steps for some time without success, stop! Try again in a few weeks or months.

For Boys Only

Many start boys seated. It minimizes extra clean up. Eventually, though, boys do stand and may need some added instruction. Aiming takes practice. When a little boy starts urinating in a standing position, be prepared to wipe up (and/or have him wipe up) around the toilet.

- Show a boy how to point his penis down to avoid spraying the room whether sitting down or standing up. (If a little girl wants to urinate standing up, explain why it doesn't work but let her try anyway if she wants to.)

34

- Teach your boy to aim accurately by having him *"sink the battleship."* Float the corner of an envelope or a piece of toilet paper in the toilet and have him aim at it. *(Cherrios also work for target practice and are flushable!)* Or float ice cubes tinted with food coloring.

- Urinating into blue *(from cleaning tablets or food coloring)* toilet bowl water will turn it green. Or add shampoo to the water and peeing will create bubbles. *(These work with girls too but it's a little harder to see.)*

- In the summertime, and in the privacy of a backyard or woods, let a boy practice his aim.

- Let fathers and sons have a *"peeing party."*

- In the winter let a boy *"write in the snow."*

- If a little boy wants to stand but needs to be a bit taller, stand behind him and let him stand on your feet.

- Be sure the toilet seat can't fall down on a young boy in these early stages. Have your child check to be sure that the seat is up securely before he urinates.

- Start teaching your son NOW that the toilet rim needs to be placed down after he's finished!

Target Training

To motivate and encourage good aim, you can purchase flushable potty targets. *Piddlers Toilet Targets* are "foam" fish made from cornstarch dyed with food coloring. *Toilet-Time Targets* are animal shapes of layered color tissue. On-line you can search under toilet targets or check The Potty Store (www.thepottystore.com) or call them toll-free at 1-866-GO-POTTY (781-848-7688) to inquire about the targets they carry.

> During my 18-month-old son's bathtime, he would pee while standing up. We gave him a plastic cup to pee into. He was able to feel in control watching what was happening and learning to stop and start. He's not ready for toilet training yet but I think we've got his attention and that's half the battle.
>
> *Teresa Fix, Carbondale, IL*
>
> My son's ability to aim had to be curtailed when he *aimed* over our balcony into the living room.
>
> *Name withheld on request*
>
> With a rubber glove and a red crayon, I drew a bull's eye in the bottom of our toilet. My two-year-old son was delighted. It made toilet training a *"hit"* rather than a *"miss"* operation.
>
> *Jolene Smith, Redlands, CA*

Dress for Success

Some parents feel that disposables are a real hindrance to toilet training. Those wonderful absorbing qualities of disposables prevent a child from feeling wet. And since children—like adults—don't enjoy this wet sensation, less absorbent diapers or pants can become a good motivator.

Going shopping with your child to buy training or "fancy" pants has often been one successful tactic. You'll probably find your child's favorite current cartoon character gracing them. Pretty ones are also available by mail from catalogs and online, as well as in stores.

Switch from diapers to pants when your child is urinating in the potty several times a day or has been dry during the day for several days. Better yet, ask your child if he or she wants to try training pants. Be flexible, though, and go back to diapers if they're more convenient for you or if the child wishes to. Some parents like to make the switch in stages, putting pants on a child for a few hours in the morning and gradually extending the time.

- For one attention-getting way to start toilet training, keep your child pantless or, if this makes you uncomfortable, in loose-fitting underpants (nylon panties for girls) with elasticized waistbands. Without diapers, many children are more motivated to go to the toilet on their own. (Plastic pants may retard "leakage" but they do make a wet diaper feel more comfortable—quite the opposite of the effect you want.) The feel of lightweight pants often help children associate the idea of elimination with the need to control it. Sensations of wet and cold are immediately obvious which is not always the case with disposables and training pants.

We were thrilled when our three-year-old was ready to wear underwear but we worried about "accidents" on our furniture. I placed a clean bathroom rug—the kind with the rubber backing—on the furniture and that became her special sitting spot. We also took her "special seat" to the homes of relatives and friends, and it helped us all to relax.

Susan Harden, Wayne, NJ

- Be sure clothing is easy to pull off and on. Avoid buttons, zippers, snaps, and belts during this period.

- Consider attaching Velcro® tabs to overalls in place of strap clips to make them easy for a child to undo.

- Take advantage of Huggies® Pull-Ups® Disposable Training Pants, Pampers®Easy Ups™, or Drypers®Next Step Training Pants. These have side stretch panels that allow children to slip them on and off like underwear. Keep in mind, that like most disposables, these don't allow the parent or child to be aware of the feeling of wetness.

- Change diapers (cloth or disposables) more frequently so a child gets use to and prefers the sensation of a dry, clean diaper.

- Or use cloth pants with a disposable pull-up over the cloth pants for protection while allowing your child to feel the wetness.

Cloth Options in Training Pants

Most of us turn to cloth training pants for that transitional time when children need to experience easy-to-remove cloth underwear that also offers extra absorbancy.

- Buy a sample cotton training pant larger than your child's present size—they often shrink—and wash them before a child wears them. If they are too tight around the legs, they will be difficult to raise and lower. Once you know which ones you and your child like, buy as many as your budget realistically allows.

- Decorate plain white cotton pants yourself using fabric paint and animal shaped sponges to stamp on designs.

- If pull-on cloth pants are too hard for your child to manage, try using a cloth diaper-wrap with Velcro® closings. Diaper wraps are absorbent, machine-washable diaper covers often including a waterproof outer layer.

There is a whole world of cloth pull-up and Velcro® closing, wrap training pants, many with waterproof outer covers for daytime or nighttime use. Brand names include Nikky, Bummis, Dappi, Bumkins, Aristocrat and Kushies/Kooshies.

While some training pants are available in stores and baby mail order catalogs, many are available from home-based businesses found on the Internet. The ones listed below also have regular catalogs available.

www.katieskisses.com	888-881-0404
www.babybunz.com	800-676-4559
www.store.yahoo.com/naturalbaby/index.html	800-388-2229
www.thebabylane.com	888-387-0019
www.borntolove.com	905-725-2559

(This last site also lists and reviews cloth diaper sites & sources.)

The One Step Ahead catalog has a few exclusive-to-them cloth diaper and training pants:

www.onestepahead.com 800-274-8440

but also check out:

The Right Start	www.rightstart.com	800-548-8531
Perfectly Safe	www.perfectlysafe.com	800-837-5437
Safe Beginnings	www.safebeginnings.com	800-598-8911
The Potty Store	www.thepottystore.com	866-GO-POTTY

Nighttime Control

When we expect children to stay dry at night we are asking them to maintain a newly learned mastery of involuntary muscles—while they are asleep! This is no easy task. It's best not to make a big deal about nighttime control for a recently daytime-trained child. If you do, the child's anxiety about the problem could delay nighttime dryness for months.

Continue using diapers at night, but praise a child who wakes up dry. Remember that failure to achieve nighttime control is not willful in young children. Developmental readiness for daytime control is not the same as developmental readiness for nighttime dryness.

It should come as no surprise that nighttime bladder control can follow daytime control by anywhere from several months to several years. Maturation is usually what brings it about. There is not much a parent can do to help a child establish nighttime control, at least until school age is reached. Doctors don't even like talking about nighttime wetting as a problem until a child is five or six years old.

Be aware that the occasional bed-wetting of preschool and early school years, and even a later return to bed-wetting, are not the same as persistent enuresis. (See page 84 for further discussion.)

My three-year-old daughter just couldn't seem to make it through the night consistently without wetting, so we're back to diapers at night only. She was so relieved when I suggested it that I felt foolish for waiting so long. She'll grow to readiness, and in the meantime, it's no big deal!
Penny Dunmire, Avonmore, PA

Helping Your Child, Practically Speaking

- Restrict fluid intake, especially before bedtime. If you haven't ended night bottles, now is probably the time to do so. Kids just drink less from cups! Don't give sweet juices or sodas (especially colas and orange soda because they contain caffeine) but don't deny a thirsty child a drink of water. Some say that going to bed thirsty just fixes a child's mind on water and increases the chances of nighttime wetting.

- Encourage your child to drink more during the daytime as

kids often don't drink enough during the day if they are in day-care and try to make up for it in the evenings.

- Have your child use the toilet just before climbing into bed. Encourage complete voiding of the bladder or have the child go back to the toilet a second time. Or encourage a child to go twice by directing him or her to void at the beginning of the bedtime process and again, just before lights out. Encouraging a child to "push" it all out also helps exercise the muscle that helps hold it all in.

- Make sure the way to the bathroom is lit, even if only with night-lights. Draw a map with your child showing the way from the bed to the bathroom to help form a visual image.

- Invest in an automatic sensor light in the bathroom that comes on automatically when someone enters the room.

- Keep the house warm enough so the child won't avoid getting up because it's too cold. You can return to energy savings later.

- Consider keeping a potty chair near your child's bed if that will make things easier.

- Practice "positive imaging" as you put your child to sleep. Help a child imagine staying dry all night and waking up dry in the morning. Talk about the pleasure of feeling dry, in control, and grown-up.

- Whisper "dry" ideas into the ear of a sleeping child. (Some psychologists say children are often receptive to such "idea planting" during certain periods of sleep.)

- Let your child know that you know that he or she will stay dry at night "soon," like other big kids. It is important to set up the expectation, but don't subject your child to heavy pressure.

- Remove diapers and replace them with training pants, cloth soakers, or disposable pull-ups only after a week or so of dry nights. Don't expect the bed to be dry if using these. Nighttime wetting can produce more urine than daytime situations.

While I was toilet training my daughter, I went into her room several times while she was asleep and gently whispered in her ear, asking her not to wet her bed. To my surprise, she awoke totally dry and eagerly ready to use her potty. For the next two days, I gave her chocolate as a reward for using the potty and continued my nightly suggestions while she slept. Gradually I stopped giving her the chocolate every time, but continued praising her for a job well done. Suddenly, she was trained (both bladder and bowel, day and night) in less than a week. But when I stopped the nighttime suggestions, she started wetting the bed again. I went back to making the suggestions, and gradually tapered off. Some may dispute the validity of this method, but for me, it worked like a charm!

Sherry Weinstein, Scotch Plains, NJ

Keeping Bedding Dry

- Wake your child to urinate before you retire. Doing this doesn't necessarily train a child, but it keeps the bed dry for some and leads to nighttime control for others. If your child is almost impossible to wake up, or becomes angry, don't try this method if under five years of age.

- Keep your child in diapers at night. Diaper pads may help, or you can line the inside of a diaper or pant with a sanitary napkin for extra absorption.

- Putting a plastic or rubber pant over a toddler-sized disposable diaper prevents leakage for some.

- Keep a flannelized rubber sheet, a plastic tablecloth, large plastic garbage bag, or a shower curtain between the sheet and the mattress before, during, and for some time after nighttime training. Protective bedding *(which goes under or over a sheet)* can be found at www.safecomfort.com/bedding.html and at www.pottytrainingsolutions.com. Rubber sheets can be found at www.bentonmedical.com/sheets.html.

- Wrap a large terry-cloth beach towel midway around the bed over a moisture barrier as mentioned above. Tuck it in at the sides and remove it if it gets wet during the night.

- Keep a sleeping bag on hand for a child to finish off a night's sleep if you are not up to changing wet sheets in the middle of the night.

- See additional ideas on page 92 and 94.

Tell a child who wakes in the night to go to the toilet whether or not he feels the need to go. Children sometimes wake up and don't know why. Impress upon your child that his body woke him up for a reason and it was probably to use the toilet.

Rena Manthei, Houston, TX

44

Chapter 4

What Do the Experts Say?

❦

One thing the experts (it's the *professional* experts we're talking about here) agree on is that you can't toilet train a child until he or she is ready—physically as well as emotionally. Another is that the age of readiness varies widely from child to child.

Most experts, including Benjamin Spock, M.D., T. Berry Brazelton, M.D., William Sears, M.D., and Penelope Leach, Ph.D., recommend waiting for the child to show signs of readiness (usually at two or later), and using suggestions instead of pressure during the training process. They all advocate rewarding success with flattery and praise.

In *Dr. Spock's Baby and Child Care* (Pocket Books), Dr. Spock's advice reflects the conventional wisdom. His recommendation is to use a potty chair for a child up to age two and a half rather than a toilet seat adapter (but to use a foot stool here if you do), but he admits that it's not a matter of critical importance. He recommends letting a child become friendly with the potty chair before introducing the idea of using it for BMs and urinating. He also adheres to the idea that the potty should not be emptied by the adult until after the child has left the room or the toilet flushed until the child loses interest in the stool before flushing, believing that for a child under two and a half it is probably too frightening. Let children play bottomless once a child has expressed a real interest but if accidents occur return to diapers. He indicates that belated back sliding on bowel control is more of a control issue causing constipation rather than the current theories that constipation is often the culprit. Spock suggests leaving nighttime training to the natural maturing of the bladder.

Dr. Brazelton's method follows a simple format. First, have your child sit (fully dressed) on a potty chair at least once a day. After that ritual is accepted, undress your child and take him or her to the potty chair. Aim for a time when your child is likely to have a bowel movement. Praise successes, but don't overdo it. If you feel your child is ready, have your child play with no clothes on from the waist down, and make it clear that it is the child's responsibility to go to the potty chair when necessary. If your child loses interest and doesn't cooperate, go back to diapers and try again in a few weeks. Brazelton has become more accepting of later training and has become a proponent of child-led, pressure-free toilet training. Emotional readiness should be the guiding factor and pressuring a child is to be avoided. He no longer considers age four to be late for training. In fact, his input was part of the reason the P & G, makers of Pampers, proceeded with developing a larger disposable diaper (size 6) for children over 35 lbs. Size 6 is now common with the major disposable diaper manufacturers.

Dr. Sears follows the basics of being sure your child is ready, that you have the tools you need ranging from a potty seat to training pants plus patience and a sense of humor, and teaching your child "where to go and what to call it." He believes in first creating a conditioned reflex that when you sit your child on the potty, your child goes. This is best done initially by catching your child's bowel movement when he or she is about to go and before it is deposited in the diaper. Make your own time chart of your child's diaper bowel movements for a week or two before starting. With successful timing, a child learns this connection and eventually makes the correct association.

John Rosemond, a family psychologist, columnist and author, believes this process should be as simple and straightforward as housebreaking a puppy. He advocates a return to traditional child rearing practices and attributes delayed training to "wishy-washy parenting inspired by Freudian mumbo jumbo." He believes the word "readiness" should really be "capable" and kids are capable of learning between 18 and 24 months of age.

Penelope Leach, Ph.D., in *Your Growing Child* (Knopf) talks about the delicate balance to be struck in toilet training between parents' need to be clear about their preference for a child to use the potty or toilet but to avoid the temptation to use toileting as a battleground. Once a child is aware of the "feeling-product" connection, a child should be told that urine and feces should be put in a potty or toilet like grown-ups do. She feels one should keep interference of a child's daily activities to a minimum. If you keep reminding a child to sit on the potty you can ruin the whole process. A potty seat's portability allows it to be brought to where the child is so a child can take responsibility yet not have to run to find a potty when muscle control can't exercise that kind of delay. Avoiding diapers is recommended and be prepared for puddles. Compliment with pleasure but don't go overboard with congratulations.

Louise Bates Ames of the Gessell Institute of Child Development sees each generation as calmer about this developmental task than its predecessor. She still recommends the use of the newspaper-on-the-bathroom-floor routine for a child (and usually a boy) who insists on squatting for a BM and refuses to use either a potty seat or the toilet until this stage passes.

A former bestselling toilet training book that has made enthusiastic converts of some and sparked controversy among others is *Toilet Training in Less Than a Day* by Nathan Azrin, Ph.D., and Richard Foxx, Ph.D., (Pocket Books, 1974). The program these two psychologists recommend was first devised not for speed, but to help the retarded learn this difficult skill. Later, it was adapted for the average child. Some people feel that the program is overly manipulative and, in some aspects, actually punitive. Others object to the heavy use of sweet drinks, sweets, and salty treats.

The demands on both parent and child are considerable. One whole day must be devoted to training, with no distractions whatsoever. The authors recommend that trainer and trainee be confined to the kitchen, where cleanup is comparatively easy. Here's a brief summary of the procedure:

1. The parent provides a doll that wets and, with prompting from the parent, the child "trains" the doll in the prescribed manner.

2. Liquids are offered constantly, on the theory that the more urine that is produced, the more quickly the training will be accomplished. Salty snacks are given freely, if necessary, to increase appetite for the liquids.

3. The parent is given a sequence of reminders to use, ranging from a firm "go now" to questions about the need to go and general suggestions.

4. The child goes to the potty, pulls down his or her pants (very loose ones are recommended), and sits there for ten minutes, or until urination occurs. The child wipes himself or herself and pulls up the pants.

5. Four rewards are given for every success: verbal praise, nonverbal reinforcement (hugs and kisses), something good to eat, and references to "friends who care" (*"Grandma will be so pleased"; "Tommy goes in the potty, too"*).

6. Disapproval is expressed when there's an accident, although "…spanking or other physical punishment is probably never justified." The child is then required to practice hurrying to

48

the potty from different places in the house 10 times (*yes, 10!*), to feel the pants in order to tell the difference between wet and dry, and finally, to do all the necessary cleanup.

But does it work? Many say it does. And in a formal study of children 20 months to four plus years of age, Azrin and Foxx found that success was achieved in periods ranging from a half hour to two days, with the average being about four hours.

Responses to a question about the method in my *Practical Parenting*™ *Newsletter* (*no longer in-print*) varied:

"*Toilet Training in Less Than a Day* was our biggest help. (My son was two years, nine months.) The two disadvantages were 1) it was very boring for me, and 2) you really should stay home for a week to be sure the method has stuck. Very much worth it."

Nancy Holte, Cannon Falls, MN

"Unless your child is eager to please you in general, the boundaries [in this book] are so rigid that you may have a major battle on your hands."

Elaine Whitlock, Northhampton, MA

"I have come to the conclusion that when your child is ready, he'll do it. I used *TTLD* for my first son when he was about three years old, and it worked! It was wonderful, and I told everyone about that book—until I tried with son No. Two, and it failed miserably! Now, seven months later, he's trained, and to this day I still don't know what caused it to happen other than that he was ready, that all the explaining, practicing—not to mention the big-boy pants with the trucks on them—finally clicked, and he understood."

Nance Don, Washington Township, NJ

Using Rewards

Toilet Training in Less Than a Day emphasizes the reward system, which has raised a major concern for parents. Many parents feel strongly that any kind of material reward is wrong or simply inappropriate when a child is learning basic proper behavior. Others don't object at all. And some object only to the use of sweets. Don't think of this as bribery. This is behavior modification.

The biggest concern of those offering rewards are, *"How and when do I stop?" "Will my child expect a treat or gift every time he or she visits the bathroom for weeks, months. . . years?"*

According to parents who have used the reward system, this is not a problem. It is easy to run out of whatever you are using after a few weeks. Kids do accept that. And a reward system can be an effective motivator!

You can differentiate rewards as you progress. When your child either asks to go without prompting (and makes it to the potty on time) or spontaneously uses the potty independently or attains a certain number of dry days, might be the time for a "larger" reward that has been previously discussed.

Use your imagination for rewards (you know your child best), and consider combining material rewards with nonmaterial ones. For some children, the most effective reward might be calling Grandpa or Grandma to report a "success" (*this obviously*

Our son would willingly pee in the toilet or potty but a bowel movement he would only do in his pants. My husband came up with the ideas of "pennies for poos"— which worked for us. It was better than sweets and boosted his bank balance. We now have a six-month-old girl and we've already started saving change!
Mary Jackson, Staten Island, NY

---

works best if grandparents live within local dialing distance!); for others, it's stickers or stars on a chart, calendar or even the potty itself. Letting your child pick out favorite stickers at a store can add to their interest. One child I know was motivated by the promise of wearing a swimsuit all day long if there were no accidents, while a set number of pushes on a swing did the trick for another child.

Placement of any tangible rewards to be handed out is helpful too. They should be in sight but out of reach. A large, clear cannister or bowl is one way to accomplish this. Or maybe having an assortment of small wrapped items stored in the bathroom.

Rewards can be a helpful incentive but they *WON'T* toilet train a child who is not *READY* to be trained. If, after a few days or a week, training is not working, forget it—rewards as well as your efforts! Back off. For some children, their egos get too wrapped up with the prize and they (as well as parents) miss the point of this exercise!

The best reward is often not a material reward at all. It is self reward! In addition to praise and pleasure expressed by adults, encourage self-praise. Teach your child to give him or herself a *"pat on the back."* Or suggest to your child *"Give yourself a hand"* so your child can self-applaud for a job well done. (*Of course, you can add to the applause too!*)

Material Rewards to Consider

- M&M Plain Chocolate Candies.

- Jelly beans, chocolate kisses, or other favorite candies.

- Sugarless candy or gum.

- Raisins: one for using the toilet, another for wiping, another for flushing, another for washing hands, etc.

- Pieces of fruit, crackers, a special cookie, or what ever treat is your child's favorite.

- A box of animal crackers—to be eaten one at a time from a box which is easily visible.

- An ice cream cone.

- A penny for each *"success"*—two, perhaps, for a bowel movement.

- A new book.

- Big-boy pants or fancy big-girl pants (or a shopping trip to get them).

- A dollar for spending in the local variety store.

- A sugarless gumball from a toy gumball machine (not for children under three years of age).

- The promise of a really grand gift (a fish, a gerbil, special toy, a trip to the zoo) after a week or two of continuous success—and then provide it right away!

"It Worked for Me"

We used a *Potty Box* with candy for rewards. A funny side effect was that the other mothers who had been so disapproving of our *Potty Box* soon noticed that their kids never had accidents when visiting us!

Lisa Smith, Hurst, TX

My mother-in-law ordered me to give M&M's as rewards for correct potty performance. Unfortunately my son responded too well and I, nine and half months pregnant at the time, was having to jump up every ten minutes to give him another chocolate and verify that he did the job. I switched to raisins, but he did not like them as much and went back to wetting his training pants. A few months later, he gradually became dry.

Lucy Tierney, Slidell, LA

I think giving candy or little gifts is very wrong. I tacked a calendar to the wall in the bathroom at his eye level. Every time he went potty, he got a star on that day. (*I bought those colored stick-on stars.*) Some days he only had two stars; other days half a dozen. It worked for us!

Linda Miner, Berkeley, CA

For rewards, we used up two boxes of Life Cereal and spent $15 on new books. I think it was cheaper than another few weeks of Pampers.

Susan Ringer, Florence, MS

Beyond Rewards

Sometimes children need that extra motivation that goes beyond buying a potty seat, verbal praise, and even rewards to remind children of what's expected.

Gentle inspiration can come in the form of books, videos, games, and even potty-training dolls. Some potty-training books may seem a bit silly to parents, but they're often adored by children because they relate to them so completely. These books demonstrate a developmental step with language and pictures a child can understand, and the characters provide role models. They clearly show what's expected of a child, which we sometimes forget to relay consistently.

Books to Read While Sitting on the Potty

For parents, books are helpful because they take some of the work off our shoulders and provide a point of departure for a casual discussion on the subject with a child.

Share the books with any caregiver who might spend time with your child. This can be grandparents, babysitters, daycare providers, or older children who read to toddlers.

Don't be surprised if potty books become a source of fascination and love to be read and reread and reread. So be sure to buy those that you can listen to repeatedly.

I read *more* books while each of my three sat on the potty chair! The books were used as a distraction. It seemed to be useless to say, *"Here's the potty, now go!"*
Nedra O'Neill, Calumet Park, IL

My favorite (*granted, I'm biased*) read-together potty book is my *KoKo Bear's New Potty* book.

KoKo Bear's New Potty
by Vicki Lansky

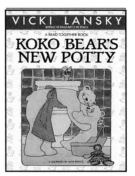

This bestselling story of KoKo Bear *(available separately or as part of the paperback edition of this book), a* unisex bear who learns to use the toilet has helped potty train thousands of children. All the steps in this growing-up process are experienced by KoKo. It lets your child know what's expected and what to expect.

There are many *(and I do mean many)* other potty books for children, each with a slightly different emphasis. So check out your book store, library or search on-line for titles such as:

Once Upon a Potty—His / Once Upon a Potty—Hers
by Alona Frankel *(HarperCollins)*
Uh Oh! Gotta Go! *Potty Tales from Toddlers*
by Bob McGrath *(Barrons)*
Going to the Potty
by Mr. Rogers *(Putnam/Paper Star)*
Everybody Poops
by Taro Gomi *(Kane/Miller)*
(Parents like this one even more than kids do.)
What to Expect When Your Child Uses the Potty
by Heidi Murkoff *(HarperCollins Juvenile)*

The list continues with:

Annie's Potty by Judith Caseley *(Greenwillow)*
Caillou—Potty Time *(Chouette Editions)*
Bye-Bye, Diapers by Ellen Weiss *(Golden Books)*
Flush the Potty by Ken Wilson-Max *(Scholastic)*
I Want My Potty by Tony Ross *(Kane/Miller)*

I Have to Go by Robert Munsch *(Annick Press)*
I'm a Potty Champion/*Book&Trophy* by Kitty Higgins (Barrons)
Max's Potty by H. Ziefert *(DK Publishing)*
My Big Boy (Big Girl) Potty by Joanna Cole
My Potty Chair by Ruth Young *(Viking Kestrel)*
On Your Potty by Virginia Miller *(Greenwillow)*
Potty Time by Langely and Civardi *(Little Simon)*
Sam's Potty by Barbro Lindgren *(Morrow)*
The Potty Chronicles by Anne Reiner *(Magination Press)*
The Potty Book for Girls (for Boys) by A. Capucilli *(Barrons)*
The Princess and the Potty by Wendy C. Lewison *(Alladin)*
Toilet Tales by Andrea W. von Konigslow *(Annick Press)*
When You've Got to Go *(Bear in the Big Blue House)*

A Free, Personalized Book on Potty Training

Huggies® Pull-Ups® offers an eight page, personalized potty book that you can print out from the Internet on your computer. *(If you place each page in a small plastic bag, it gives the book longevity. Or laminate the pages.)* It prints in black and white, or color and can be for a boy or a girl. You choose hair and skin color and input your child's name. Go to:

www.pull-ups.com/storybook/selections.asp

Should You Need More Inspiration...

Videos

If books are not your medium, maybe videos are. The best place to find them is on Amazon.com under video or baby or Toys 'r Us. Then read the comments by those who have purchased them to help you decide what is of interest to you.

Once Upon A Potty **for Him...***Once Upon a Potty* **for Her**
Barron's Home Video   *800-645-3476*
These videos are the animated and expanded versions of
the book of the same name by Alona Frankel. 30 minutes.
Potty Time with Bear (*Bear in the Big Blue House*)
For children. 25 minutes. VHS.

It's Potty Time
Learning Through Entertainment   *800-237-6889*
For children two and over. Endorsed by Duke University
Medical Center. Uses songs and a story about a birthday
party to teach the steps for toilet training and washing up.
25 minutes. VHS. Also available with a hardcover book and
a singing teddy bear. (www.lteinc.com)
Let's Go Potty
Live action video. 22 minutes VHS.
The Potty Project
Developed by a pediatrician, it encourages very small
children to learn the basics of toilet training.
Winston's Potty Chair
A cartoon video produced in cooperation with the AMA.

...or even a Doll!

One very effective concept that many parents have used is
letting their child toilet train a doll or stuffed animal. Many a
teddy bear has paved the way to successful use of the toilet.

Dolls that wet and are ready for toilet training include *Baby
Alive* from Kenner, and *Betsy Wetsy, Tiny Tears* and *Magic Potty
Baby* from Tyco Toys.

But should you prefer to have a doll straight from the pages
of a potty book, *(as you can see on the next page)* you can.

KoKo Bear Potty Package
— a Book and a Buddy —

KoKo Bear's New Potty book comes to life with an 8" plush bear dressed in a purple t-shirt, Velcro® diapers, pull-up pants and a bathroom back-drop for role playing.

Package (KoKo book/doll/backdrop)
$17.95 + s/h
Practical Parenting/Book Peddlers
www.practicalparenting.com (go to toilet training)
Also at www.amazon.com (ISBN 0-916773-69-8)

KoKo Doll *(alone)*
$12.95 +s/h
Doll comes with t-shirt, Velcro®-closing diaper & pull-up pants. Available alone only by mail from *Practical Parenting/Book Peddlers (800-255-3379)*

Chapter 5

Help! How Can I Toilet Train My Uncooperative Child?

❦

The standard line offered to the parent of a child who's hard to train is, "No child has gotten on the school bus in a diaper yet." This, of course, is not much help if you are trying to figure out how to proceed.

If your child has progressed from the terrible twos to the formidable fours without showing the slightest interest in the toilet, your concern is justified. If your child prefers to squat, comfortably diapered, in a dark corner, holding a special blanket, you may be dealing with physical or emotional complications, irrational fears, or ingrained habit. You may have a willful child who needs some special handling, or you may be dealing with a simple problem in semantics.

It's also possible that your timing is off. Asynchrony is a big word that simply means that a child's "internal clock" is set differently from those of other members of the family. Elimination may not occur when you think it should. For example, a child

59

may have only one bowel movement in two days, or three in one day. If this is the case, it's you who will have to do the adjusting.

And, painful but true, you yourself may be causing the trouble. Ask yourself the questions listed in the box below. If you have two or three "yes" answers, perhaps you should sit back and do a little thinking. Try talking out your problems with your spouse, a friend, a doctor, or nurse practitioner—but *don't* take your frustrations out on your child.

Some Questions to Ask Yourself

- Are you determined to have your child toilet trained by a certain age or stage in his or her life, or at some special point in your own?

- Do you see your life as being in a shambles until your child is trained?

- Are you particularly sensitive to pressure from family or friends to "get that child to use the toilet"?

- Do you think your child is punishing you by not cooperating with your training efforts?

- Are you positive that because your child can understand you there's no reason toilet training can't be accomplished easily?

- Have you ever been described as a "controlling" parent?

- Are you strongly opposed to backing off for now and trying again in a month, when all the pieces might fall into place?

One possible solution might be to have someone else take over. Sometimes, for all our good intentions, we are simply too emotionally involved to get the job done. Some parents can't teach their own teenagers to drive, and wisely turn the task over to someone who's better able to deal with it unemotionally. This doesn't mean they're bad parents. In fact, they're to be congratulated for recognizing the problem and taking the proper steps to correct it. It's the same with toilet training. If you can see that the process is getting you too upset, and that you, in turn, are upsetting your child, try to find someone else with some emotional distance who can do it for you. And don't feel guilty! Part of being a good parent is knowing what you can and can't do. You won't prove anything by trying to do the impossible.

Physical Complications

If you suspect that it's a physical problem, have your child checked thoroughly by a physician.

- Consider the possibility of an allergy. Lactose intolerance (the inability to digest milk or milk products) is the most common, but other foods can cause allergies, too.

- How much sorbitol is your child consuming in sugarless candies and gum? Sorbitol is a new culprit in chronic loose stools. It also is found naturally in pear juice and apple juice which could make a difference if a child drinks lots.

- Watch for signs of urinary infections. These include pain or burning sensations while urinating, straining to urinate, color changes in the urine, foul-smelling urine, frequent urination that produces very little, or a split stream of urine. Other signs could be abdominal pain or a fever of an undetermined origin. Such infections are not uncommon in small children.

- Be aware that even after a urinary problem has cleared up, the child may still remember and fear the pain of urinating, and this may complicate potty training. Reassure the child and don't be impatient if it takes him or her a while to get over the fear.

My daughter at age four would often have accidents—to my distress. I thought she was being lazy and refusing to stop her play to take the time to go to the bathroom which she knew how to do. I was on her case a lot. At our annual physical, we discovered it was a physical problem. My guilt load was heavy for a long time.
Martha Berk, Louisville, KY

- Check a toilet trained child who starts to have many urinary accidents, as well as a significant increase in urination for diabetes.

- Remember that diarrhea—persistent runny, loose stools can cause problems with bowel control. Persistent diarrhea is usually a symptom of a physical problem, and it should be treated by a doctor.

- Consider the possibility that constipation (see page 29) is keeping your child from wanting to move his or her bowels, because it is painful. If it's not chronic, you can help by keeping the children company while they're sitting on the toilet, lubricating the anus with Vaseline, or even helping hold the "cheeks" apart to make it easier to move the bowels. Dietary changes can also help. Chronic constipation can put pressure on the bladder and cause daytime, as well as nighttime, accidents in which case it's time to seek medical attention.

Emotional Complications

Don't hesitate to seek professional help if you think there's an emotional problem you can't solve. Getting help from a therapist doesn't mean that your child is in serious trouble, and you may find that things improve rapidly after only a session or two. Children are often more open with a neutral third party person than with a parent. Remember that children often keep silent about fear or shame they're feeling. Therapists are trained to help children learn to express and deal with these feelings.

- Remember that the emotional makeup of a human being is extremely complex. It's not realistic to expect that just because a child is small in stature, he or she will have a small range of emotions. And handling all these strange feelings and sensations is doubly hard for a child because of his or her undeveloped wisdom and lack of information.

- Watch for interference from others. Siblings can set a child off by playing on fears and expectations; friends or even teachers may say the wrong thing.

- Ask your child to show you how he or she would toilet train a doll or stuffed animal. Watch the child's behavior and listen carefully to commands and instructions. If the child uses abusive language, scolds, and handles the toy roughly, it might be a clue that your own or someone else's attitudes and actions are at fault.

- Or get the child to draw a picture of a bathroom. Ask for explanations of anything you don't understand. You may get some clues about worries or fears the child has been repressing.

Toilet Fears

Some children—especially those with older, storytelling siblings—believe the toilet is a hiding place for sharks, alligators, or water monsters. The sound of a toilet flushing may serve to confirm this. One mother on discovering that her child feared the monsters in the toilet, led her child to the bathroom, called the monsters up out of the toilet, and blew them out the window, much to the child's relief.

Don't flush the toilet while the child is still sitting on it. Many children find the noise and action frightening and worry about being "swallowed up." Showing a child how things work inside the toilet tank and taking the child to the basement to explain the workings of the plumbing system may banish this fear.

Willfulness

If you have a truly willful child, you will have seen stubbornness and other signs before now. They don't usually begin to appear just at this time. If you have seen the signs before, look back and remember how you've handled your stubborn child who sometimes digs in his or her heels and refuses to cooperate.

Sometimes a three- or four-year-old child stubbornly refuses to make a bowel movement in the toilet or potty and insists on diapers even when the child uses the potty or toilet appropriately when urinating. Sometimes a child even insists on taking underwear off and putting a diaper on just before a BM. It's frustrating because it's obvious the child feels the sensation of the coming BM and can exercise control to go when he or she wants to. In addition, children who retain BMs for any great length of time are more likely to become constipated. Sitting a child on the toilet for long periods is not necessary when a child understands how to use the toilet. Children who have been lectured or reminded too often, and forced to sit on the toilet for long periods of time against their will, may understandably be resistant to your pressure when control is the issue.

There is no single solution to this situation. For a child who might be stuck in this behavior and for whom even rewards don't work, and you don't think constipation (as described on page 29) is the problem, change your approach. Back off for a few weeks. Wait for a stress-free week, and then tell your child that when this box of diapers is gone you're not having any more diapers. Transfer all responsibility to your child explaining that *"It's your job to make your BM and get it into the toilet. You no longer need my help."* Explain also that it's okay if your child has a BM or wets but he or she can't walk around in soiled underwear. Clean clothes must be worn before engaging in any other activity.

You can also :

- Consider using reverse psychology: *"Oh, I'm sure you won't want to use the potty today: we'll just put the diaper on."* Or switch roles: *"I need to go potty. Will you keep me company?"*

- Avoid "no" answers as much as possible by telling your child *"It's time to try"* instead of asking *"Do you have to go?"*

- Give choices: *"Do you want to help get your pants off and wipe yourself, or should I do it?" "Do you want to use the potty chair today or the big toilet?"*

- Physically lead the child to the toilet with a hand on a shoulder or arm, not roughly, but firmly enough so the child knows you mean business.

- Increase unconstipating foods (see page 29) at mealtime. Keep a matter-of-fact attitude in the face of tantrums and accidents, and show no annoyance.

- Think of your child just as a "late bloomer" to help you avoid feeling frustrated.

- Discuss this with your child's day-care provider as it may provide additional insights and offer you both new ways to handle this problem.

At age three my son refuses to have BMs on the potty. He insists on a diaper. I've pinpointed the problem—he just can't "perform" sitting down! On one hand, he becomes very upset if he does go in his pants, but if I suggest he sit on the potty, he insists he "can't." He had no trouble learning to urinate.

Sandra Heath, Brownsville, TX

- Completely back off. Possibly your style and your child's temperament are working against each other.

Chapter 6

How Can I Toilet Train a Child Under Special Circumstances?

❦

Sometimes toilet training must be attempted under conditions that are less than ideal, regardless of our preferences.

You start training a month before the new baby is expected, and then the baby comes three weeks early! Or training is progressing slowly, and you're only halfway there, three days before the family leaves for a long vacation.

You didn't opt for twins, but twins you have—and both are ready and eager to be trained at the same time. Maybe your day-care center started training procedures just before you are about to leave for a vacation. Or jury duty calls!

The greatest challenge is probably the one presented to parents of a child who is physically or developmentally challenged or one who will ultimately be diagnosed as dyslexic. Severe problems such as these will require the advice and cooperation of your physician. Your physician will be able to give you information, resources and suggest reading material that will be helpful. Drs. Azrin and Foxx, the authors of *Toilet Training in Less Than a Day* have worked with those who have disabilities of one kind or another and have also written *Toilet Training for the Retarded* (Research Press, 1973).

The New-Baby Syndrome

If you have a choice, you probably won't want to start training a child just before or after the birth of a new baby. Before the birth, you won't be up to the running, and after the birth, you'll probably be too busy. So start several months before or several months after the fact. Remember your older child is going to see how much attention your new baby will be getting in activities like diapering and sometimes an older child just likes to regress to babyhood for desired attention. Wait until the baby is old news. But if you must go ahead with it, think about these things.

- Plan to give the child a great deal of attention. Take no shortcuts. Spend a lot of time alone with the child and do everything you can to set comfort and self-assurance levels as high as possible. *(Easy to say, I know.)*

- Involve your spouse or someone else in the process so your attention alone is not the sole motivating factor!

- Emphasize the grown-up aspects of being toilet trained, and choose whatever status symbols ("grown-up pants," treats) or other rewards you wish.

- If after two weeks you see few signs of success, postpone toilet training until you're sure your child is ready for it. Do not make the child feel guilty for "failing." (See *Regression*, page 82.)

> Leah, almost two, couldn't have chosen a worse time. I was nearly due with my third child and I knew siblings sometimes regress when a baby is born. I thought she should wait but she disagreed! I explained my theory of privilege and responsibility. *"If you want your diaper off, you must use the potty."* (To this day I'd rather deal with a messy diaper than messy pants.) She had to convince me—and she did. Her one accident seemed tragic to her and was never repeated.
>
> *Lois Slusky, Ferndale, MI*

Working Parents

With most young mothers returning to work within three to twelve months after having a baby, toilet training today is often done by, or in conjunction with a childcare provider. Obviously, every caretaker (be it an in-house sitter, a home day care provider, or someone at a day-care center) will have her (or his) own style. Since there is no one magic way to train a child, working parents will need to integrate their system with the one a child is exposed to during the day.

A study released in 2001 by the Medical College of Wisconsin found no correlation between children's toilet training completion and whether they are in day-care or have mothers who work outside the home.

If you are comfortable with the general discipline, style, and attitude of the environment your child is exposed to, the odds are you will also be comfortable with the system or process used for toilet training. Toilet training philosophies and techniques should be part of the interview process, especially if you are interviewing a childcare provider when your child is 12 to 18 months of age.

Nursery schools (versus a day-care center) for children three and up usually require children to be toilet trained because of licensing requirements.

Day-care Dynamics

Group day-care will provide a different dynamic from training one-on-one at home, but the principles are basically the same. One advantage of group day-care is that peer pressure often speeds up the process.

- Start good two-way communications before the process begins. Parents may want to begin training, but it is often the caregiver who may first see the signs of readiness. Tell your child's caregivers *before* you start toilet training, and ask them to do likewise. Some centers use the process of checking a child every half hour or watching for consistently dry periods of time every day, to use as an indication of readiness.

- Consider introducing toilet training for two weekends before the day-care provider begins. If it can be arranged, you might take some vacation days to at least get the process started at home.

- Using the same language and having the same attitude toward toilet training makes the adjustment from one environment to the other smoother and less confusing for your child. Also, if a reward system is used, make sure it's consistent between home and day-care.

- To keep the issue a priority, make sure you and your provider are in the habit of reminding your child about the various aspects of toilet training using similar language in questions such as, *"Are you dry now?"* or *"Do you have to go to the potty?"*

- Bring at least five changes of clothes and underwear to your child's day-care site every day during this process. Your child

WILL have accidents and shouldn't be reduced to wearing a diaper by the end of the day.

- Check which kind of potty chair is used at your child's center as it might influence your method of training at home. Many centers, however, have very low, flushable child-sized toilets. (Also, find out if they use foot stools at the center.)

- Try to increase your fun time together after work before getting down to the business of toilet training if your quality time together is limited.

- Remember to dress your child in easy access clothes. It's probably not a good time to use overalls.

- Show an interest in your child's experiences using the potty at day-care by talking about them together.

- Be prepared to back off if your child does not show progress within two to four weeks or any agreed upon arrangement with your childcare provider. Sometimes they're just not ready regardless of perceived readiness.

- Be aware that some children who use the toilet appropriately at the center may not bother to do so at home. This is not an uncommon occurrence though usually just a temporary one.

Traveling During Training

Travel may or may not interfere with training. On a short trip, it probably won't; on a longer one, it may. Don't make your trip a battleground. You can work on toilet training when you get home.

Some children love the idea of a strange toilet, while others will absolutely refuse to use one. And, most frustrating, the same child may demonstrate both attitudes within a couple of months.

- If you anticipate extensive travel, consider opting for the adult toilet seat for toilet training rather than a potty chair. It will simplify your packing.

- Look into the purchase of travel-style adapters that fit into your bag such as the folding-style seat adapter featured on pages 20.

I explained to my daughter that the diaper I put on her was to be used only as a last resort, that she should tell me when she had to go, and we would try to find a restroom. This did not set back her toilet training at all. In fact, the few times when she did have to use the diaper, she was upset that she couldn't use a "big-girl potty." This phase lasted only a few months until she learned to control her bladder.

Cheryl Shephard, Brecksville, OH

- Try to know the location of an acceptable rest room before you need it. For instance, when entering a museum check out the floor plan for restroom locations. With last minute announcements, little ones can't wait very long.

- Condition your child to the idea of using a variety of toilets in strange places by doing just that before your trip. Take the child into gas-station and department store restrooms; visit bathrooms in friends' homes and in restaurants. If you will be vacationing out-of-doors, practice those *"au natural"* methods.

- Take advantage of larger handicap booths when available to you so there is more room for you and your child.

- Explain how the bathroom on a train or airplane will look and sound.

- Pack a waterproof sheet or felt-back plastic tablecloth to go under the sheet to protect mattresses from an accident or leaking diapers. Even large plastic garbage bags will do.

- Pack some disposable diapers just in case your best-laid plans go awry. Trips are more important than momentary setbacks in toilet training.

Our two-year-old was going through potty training while her older siblings were being driven to scouts, baseball practice, etc. She was afraid of the regular toilet so I'd bring her potty chair in the car with a small plastic garbage bag to line the potty chamber (*plus toilet paper*) **and she'd always use her portable "out house." Afterwards I'd lift out the bag, tie and dispose of it. We never had wet pants!**
Linda Mahoney, Broomfield, CO

Car Conveniences

No matter what you use enroute, do stop the car and pull over to the side when your child has to go.

- Carry a wide-mouth bottle, a large disposable, lidded soft drink cup, a coffee can or plastic ice-cream pail with a lid (*that can also be used for motion sickness*) for a child to urinate in. Any of these can also be used by a girl, if she sits tightly on the rim.

- Consider filling any of these containers halfway with the absorbent stuffing from a disposable diaper. It avoids "sloshing." In fact, for a boy urinating, all you need is a large resealable plastic bag stuffed with a disposable diaper or paper towels.

- Carry a potty chair or portable camping potty with you on a car trip.

Au Natural

Boys have the advantage out-of-doors when going behind a bush or the like. A girl needs help squatting and keeping her pants out of the way. If privacy permits, remove pants altogether. If squatting is problematic, crouch behind her, holding her out with your hands holding her bent knees and your elbows cradling her hips. Regardless, do carry diaper wipes for clean-ups of hands as well as bottoms.

As a pediatric nurse practitioner, I advise parents to accompany a child until they're around seven. Although mothers can take a boy into a ladies' room, fathers should not take a girl into a men's room, since urinals are not private. A father should ask a woman to escort his daughter while he waits outside.

Meg Zweiback, R.N., P.N.P., Oakland, CA

Using Public Restrooms Alone

The question of when to allow a child to use public toilet facilities unsupervised is a serious concern though parents seldom compare notes on this subject. Unfortunately this is a safety issue, and a real one at that. Once children (four to six years of age) prefer their own privacy and understand the differences between the mens' room and the ladies' room, you do need to respect their need for a same-sex facility. Most parents don't usually allow this to be a completely independent procedure until a child is over seven.

Women's rooms offer more privacy than those in men's rooms so it is more appropriate for children to come in with mom than it is to use the restroom with dad.

Always be prepared for facilities to be out of toilet paper. Carry purse-size tissue packages with you. Alert your child to check the toilet paper rolls first and to come to you ahead of time if none is available in any stall.

Despite the unkept appearance of some public restrooms, it is highly unlikely that any disease can be contracted from a toilet seat. Wiping a seat dry is adequate even when not aesthetically pleasing. Washing hands afterwards is, however, doubly important.

Supervised

- Stand outside the door while your child uses the facilities alone.

- Ask an appropriate-looking man to take a boy into the restroom while you wait outside the door. (*Same for situations with girls, Dad.*)

- Only let a child go alone to one that is in shouting distance or in view.

Unsupervised

Can your child perform all the necessary tasks alone from locking the door to flushing to washing hands? Does your child have a healthy suspicion of strangers? If so, then it's time to let an interested child go alone. But still be alert to your child's whereabouts.

- Keep track of the amount of time your child is gone.

- Let two children go together.

Some restrooms are never safe. Use your judgment and let your children understand your standards and why. A child could use a familiar family-style restaurant restroom alone at a young age but should not be allowed to visit a bathroom in an out-of-the-way store facility.

This is a very difficult issue for me because of a rare, fatal case of abduction from a store's basement bathroom that occurred in our community. Francesca, age five, insists on going to the bathroom alone. I stand outside, making sure there is only one entrance. I don't want to make my daughter nervous but she knows that if it's crowded or if anything she doesn't like happens to her, she's to *"come out and get mom,"* or just call out for me.

Nancy Tuminelly, Richfield, MN

Toilet Training Twins

Given the laundry or cost of disposables, there is the added economic incentive here to toilet train twins sooner. But their readiness, like singletons, is variable and usually later than our readiness. Some parents try to avoid training them at the same time, holding one off in any way possible, and others believe in plunging in and getting it all over at once.

Some people say that twins are not usually developmentally ready for toilet training until a little later than singletons are, but others disagree. There's such wide variation among children that the point has little validity anyway. When they're ready, they're ready.

Fraternal twins may vary as much in readiness as any other two children of the same age, with a boy likely to be ready somewhat later than a girl. Even identical twins may be ready weeks or months apart.

Sometimes problems arise with twins when one is both physically and emotionally ready for training and the other is not, but wants (or even demands) to share the experience. If you can manage to train them singly, even months apart, be grateful, and enjoy having just one in diapers.

- If you're training two at the same time, make things as easy as possible on yourself by moving gradually from diapers to training pants. Try pants for just a few hours a day, and when all of you are tired, change to diapers.

- Concentrate on treating the twins as individuals, not as a matched pair. Never compare the progress of one against the other. Don't impose one child's readiness on the other by comparing or blaming.

- Keep expressions of pleasure for the successes of one child low key enough so as not to set up competition for affection. And rewarding the successes of just one twin may cause the other to be resentful rather than to be motivated. It will probably work best if both are rewarded for the successes of just one. There's a better chance both will be encouraged to try harder.

- Boys can share a toilet while urinating but with it will also come the tears and tantrums from the inevitable wetting of one by the other.

- Take advantage of the fact that a trained twin will be a perfect role model when the second is ready.

- Supply two potty chairs, in different colors, and assign one very specifically to each twin. It's not reasonable to expect that there won't be times when both have to use the potties at the same time. Some parents feel that you should allow no switching or you may have a tantrum on your hands.

- For twins who like doing EVERYTHING together, even after one or both can use the adult toilet, you may need to keep one potty chair in the bathroom awhile longer.

> I think I deserve the reward for potty training twins. If one
> of them wasn't running to the bathroom, I was.
>
> *Robyn Neuman, Beaver Dam, WI*

Separation from a Parent

If you have been the primary toilet trainer and anticipate being
absent during part of the process, you should prepare your child
and do some follow-up while you're gone.

- Suggest to the other parent or whoever will be carrying on the
  process that this book be required reading, at least mark
  significant passages. Prepare the person who will be in charge
  with tips and your observations on how best to handle things.

- Explain in simple language that you will be gone for a while,
  but that everything else will be the same (if it will; do prepare
  him or her for any changes you know about). Don't make a big
  deal of the absence. Promise to bring back something special
  for the child and then do it!

- Try to telephone while you're gone. Casually ask if your child
  has been going to the toilet as usual. If the answer is *"yes,"*
  express your delight. If the answer is *"no,"* tell the child you
  hope it will be *"yes"* the next time you call.

- If your child regresses when you return, don't show disap-
  pointment or promote shame.

Chapter 7

What If My Already-Trained Child Has Accidents?

❦

Becoming toilet trained is like learning to walk. It happens in fits and starts, two steps forward and one step back. Even among fully trained children, accidents can *(and often do)* happen. Occasional accidents are part of the toilet training process. Frequent accidents, however, may be an indicator that your child is not quite ready.

Moments of great excitement or fear, absorption in play, or a bad dream can be the cause of an occasional accident. Illness, stress of any kind, or jealousy of an infant sibling may bring on repeated accidents or even real regression.

Fear of using a strange toilet can be the reason behind an accident, with a child choosing the lesser of two evils.

Accidents

- Consider the possibility of an undiagnosed illness or an allergic reaction to certain foods or beverages (milk and milk products are often culprits), if your child has repeated unexplained accidents, or can't stay dry for two hours. Check with your doctor.

- If your child is ill, expect accidents until he or she has recovered enough to regain control.

- Don't punish a child for an accident. Clean up in a matter-of-fact way, help the child change clothes if necessary, and say no more about it.

- Use language like, *"I know you wanted to go in the potty but you just had an accident. Don't feel sad. You'll get better at this."*

- Don't be surprised if your child feels worse than you do about an accident. Your main job might be to console him or her. A child who's anxious to please may agonize over what he or she sees as "shameful" behavior. You might tell your child about one of your own early accidents, if you think it will help.

- Encourage the child to go to the potty after the accident "just to see if there's any more." (*There often is*).

- Don't allow siblings to tease a child for accidents.

I made a big deal out of the trip to the store with my three-year-old when he indicated he wanted Superman pants and agreed that he would keep the underpants dry. He had a couple of accidents but he was really trying. The next day he had only one accident and after that, no more wet pants. He wet and had bowel movements in the toilet from then on. I have to add that my son is very stubborn and I didn't think toilet learning was going to be easy but it was.
Beverly McMillan, Scappoose, OR

Deliberate "Accidents"

Most children can't perform at will, but sometimes a child who is able to tries to punish or threaten a parent with this powerful weapon. *"Give me _____ or I'll _____ ..."* and *"Stop talking on the phone or I'll _____ ..."* are good attention getters.

- Don't overreact. This is not the time to give the attention that's so desperately desired.

- Do say that it's the child's ACT that disappoints you or makes you angry. (Be sure the child knows you still love him or her.)

- Don't rush to help the child get cleaned up. An already-trained child has learned to be uncomfortable in wet or soiled pants, and a little discomfort now may help to prevent repeat performances.

- Have the child help you clean the floor and rinse out his

or her pants, and remember that an *especially* good job of handwashing will be required afterward. (A quick bathtub clean-up is sometimes needed too.)

• Enforcing the rule of clean clothing needs to be the parent's responsibility. Soiled clothing will require adult assistance while wet ones can usually be handled by a child alone.

Later, be sure your child gets plenty of love and attention, and be generous with praise for every example of good behavior.

I thought Eric would never quit having accidents. Finally on his fourth birthday he said, "Mom, I'm four now and I'm not going to mess my pants any more." And except for occasional night accidents, he hasn't!
Jessica Murray, Ventura, CA

Regression

Regression (*back to square one!*) may seem, at first to be simply a series of accidents, but it goes on . . . and on. It's more likely to have an emotional cause than a physical one, and it's most likely to occur during a period of stress: a new baby in the family, a death, separation from a parent. It may last for some time. If there is regression for any reason, lack of elimination control will probably be the first symptom.

• If regression is total and lasts more than a week or so, give up and go back to diapers.

• Realize that a jealous child is trying to compete with a new baby on its own level. Play up the boring and the unappealing aspects of infancy while stressing the advantages of being older.

- Casually suspend some "big-boy/big-girl" privileges—the later bedtime, some grown-up foods, certain television programs—and show surprise if the child complains. More important, do try to spend as much time as possible alone with the child.

- Try to get to the bottom of any other worry you suspect is a cause of regression. Help a child work through grief or explain a separation in terms the child can understand. Children often suffer from guilt when bad things happen, thinking they are to blame.

- Have your child help you clean up as much as is realistic, but don't shame or scold.

- Go back to toilet training when you think the child is ready for it *(he or she may very well tell you)*, but don't make references to "the first time." This is a fresh start.

- Have someone else take over the major part of the retraining, if possible, to enhance the relief of that fresh start. And don't feel like a failure or a bad parent if you do this. In fact, you should be proud of yourself for recognizing a problem and doing something positive.

> **After spending one miserable week being involved with my two and one half-year-old's accidents, I simply asked him if he still wanted to be in diapers. He said yes, and so he wore them for a few more weeks. Later, he came to me and said, *"Mommy, no more diapers."* I am beginning to learn that I do not want the power (not that you can ever have it) over my child's "self."**
>
> *Mrs. B. Leckart, Los Angeles, CA*

Regression may surface only for nighttime bed-wetting for the little older child. It can be a subconscious call for attention.

Chapter 8

How Can I Deal with Bed-Wetting?

❦

Bed-wetting is not considered to be a real problem (it's called *enuresis*) by most pediatric heath care providers until after a child is five or six years old. It may happen occasionally or every night. While it's distressing and frustrating for parents, you should bear in mind that a third of children over three and 25% of those over four lack nighttime control. Even by ages six to seven, one child in seven wets while sleeping. Estimates are that five to seven million children over the age of six wet their beds regularly. Small comfort—but at least you're not alone!

Remind yourself, every time you have to face a wet bed, that no child *wants* to be a bed-wetter. Your child's desire for night-time control is probably greater than yours. It's been said by many, but it bears repeating:

A child should never be punished for wetting the bed.

Bed-wetting is not deliberate nor is it an act of laziness. It is less of a learned skill and more of a physiological development. Nighttime control is largely involuntary. Often control can be learned through behavior modification techniques alone or in conjunction with other help but often, even with help, patience is needed. For some children, just the body maturation of preadolescence removes the problem. It is said that 15% of bed-wetting children get over the problem without treatment each additional year as they mature.

Some Possible Causes for Bed-wetting

- Deep sleep may make it impossible for many children to respond to body signals. Some call it "arousal dysfunction" because you don't wake up to normal stimuli of a full bladder.

- Lack of awareness, even in a light sleeper.

- Heredity. If family members have been prone to bed- wetting, a child often is too. If one parent was a bed wetter then a child has a 50% chance of doing so. If both parents were, then there is a 75% chance that a child will be, too.

- Stress caused by changes in a child's life or illness.

- Constipation, which can inhibit bladder capacity. (See page 29.)

- Allergy to milk, which may be tested by removing all milk products from the child's diet for several weeks. (A calcium supplement may be recommended by your physician). Other food sensitivities may also be involved.

- Illness (especially if treated with drugs) during which usual nighttime control may be lost and not regained for some time after recovery.

- Urinary tract infections, especially if the child is a girl.

- Small bladder capacity and / or an irritable bladder is believed by some to be a cause for bed-wetting problems.

- Sickle-cell anemia, one symptom of which may be the inability to stay dry all night. (This disease is common in children of color.)

My husband and friends can't believe that I wet the bed until I was 11 but it's true. My sister did also until she was 10 and my brother until he was seven. I can remember all of those mornings waking up being spanked while I was still sleeping because I had wet the bed. At a physical, the doctor told my father to spank us because we were just too lazy to get up in the night. NOT TRUE. I never once felt the sensation of having to go to the bathroom while sleeping. I wish I knew who that doctor was. I'd give him a piece of my mind.

Elaine Arter, O'Fallon , MO

I have been living with this problem with my daughter who just turned seven on and off for about three years. She had a full 18 months of being dry though I now believe it was probably because of the medicine she was taking for her bronchitis. We are working on this together now because she wants to be dry all the time. However, I have come to realize that parents can be too accepting which denies the child's desire to solve the problem. From what I've read 96% of children who wet when they sleep are simply DEEP SLEEPERS. The way to solve the problem is to break the deep sleep pattern. When we'd take her to the bathroom at night, we'd try to wake her—no zombie trips. Using an alarm belt, she was able to break the cycle in a few months and it's never been a problem since.

Teri Hay, Lancaster, PA

Helping Your Child, Psychologically Speaking

- Remember that punishing, scolding, and embarrassment have been proven NOT to help a child achieve nighttime control. Don't use these methods!

- Take your child to the doctor for a check-up just in case there's a physical cause for the bed-wetting. Seldom, however, is the problem physical. Still this will assure both you and the child that everything possible is being done.

- Be sure to tell your children that you know that they are not doing this on purpose, and that the problem doesn't make you love or admire them any less. Refer to them only as "accidents."

- Don't let siblings tease a child.

"Mom! Theron's dried his bed again."

- Explain to a son that bed-wetting is twice as common in boys than girls and that he is definitely not the only boy with this problem.

- Let your child know that disposable pants (no need to call them diapers) can be a realistic option until this period passes. Let him or her know that plenty of adults wear such items during the day as well as at night.

- Practice positive imaging. Help a child relax at bed-time and imagine waking up dry. Doctors are using this form of treatment with much success, especially with children six years and older. Also try whispering encouraging words to your child while he or she is sleeping.

- Explain to your child, using simple language, that he or she is experiencing a maturational delay and that there is nothing seriously wrong. This problem is outgrown by 99% of the population. *(Don't mention that the "cure" often comes with the onset of puberty.)*

- Offer rewards for nighttime control as you have for daytime toilet training (see *Rewards*, page 50). The use of progress charts with stars or check marks is often a helpful motivator. There is one you can use or photocopy at the end of this book. *(If you reproduce it, enlarge it.)* Also ask your child for ideas for rewards.

- Consider professional counseling if secondary enuresis occurs—that is bed-wetting by a child who has been considered nighttime trained (dry at night for four to six months) but begins to wet again. If a medical reason can't be found, it may be suggested that you look for a psychological one.

- Hypnotherapy is an option for some children.

> **I assure my five and eight year old that this won't go on forever and that they should think of their brain as a computer that has a short circuit to their bladder. Meanwhile their bodies are growing and someday their brain will make the connection and it will stop.**
>
> *Chris Young, Fallbrook, CA*

Practically Speaking

Not everyone agrees that all of these ideas work, but for many they have.

- Work on bladder-stretching exercises. Have your child hold his or her urine during the day as long as possible. Starting and stopping the stream of urine may also increase muscle control. Kegel exercises can strengthen bladder muscles, too.

- Have your child lie down on a bed in a sleeping position and "hold back" as long as possible before urinating. Practice at this will help a child learn to recognize body signals while lying down.

- Restricting fluid intake before bedtime, some believe will help; others feel it's best to have EXTRA fluids so bladder fullness is easier to notice. Certainly never let a child go to bed thirsty. Do avoid carbonated and caffeine drinks. Caffeine is a powerful diuretic that increases urine production. Eliminate milk products after noontime, if you suspect or see a causal relationship. Some children need to go off milk completely but don't do that for more than a few days without your doctor's supervision.

- Constipation, if an issue, can press on a bladder during the night causing bed-wetting.

- Encourage your child to drink more during the day (kids often forget and tend to drink more in the evenings to make up not drinking during the day) and then you can limit intake in the late afternoon and evening.

- Be sure a child goes to the bathroom before going to bed at least once if not twice.

- Make sure pajamas are easy to remove. Have extra ones easily available.

- Is the way to the bathroom lit? Night lights plugged in to all available outlets are an inexpensive investment.

- Wake your child up before YOU go to bed, taking him or her to the bathroom. It might help and should at least reduce some of the bladder's contents. (Some feel, however, this fosters a dependency on parents that interferes with the task the child must learn alone.)

- Pinpoint the time your child tends to wet the bed and set an alarm clock to go off about one hour before. Make it the child's responsibility to get up and go to the bathroom. This isn't a cure all but it will give a child more dry waking days which will be encouraging.

- Contact your local children's hospital, behavioral pediatrics clinic or sleep disorder center, as many now offer enuresis counseling.

Going by the Book

Check out what others have written on this topic if you are feeling frustrated. Each one may have something to offer that you haven't considered before. There is:

> *A Parent's Guide to Bed-Wetting Control* by Azrin and Besalel *(Pocket Books)* deals with the bell and pad method.

Waking Up Dry: How to End Bedwetting Forever by M. Scharf, Ph.D. *(Writer's Digest, 1986)*.

No More Bed-wetting: How to Help Your Child Stay Dry by Dr. S. J. Arnold *(John Wiley, 1997)*.

Getting to Dry by Maizels, Rosenbaum & Keating *(Harvard Common Press, 1999)* who run the Chicago Children's Memorial Hospital program, *"Try for Dry"*.

And for inspiration and support for children, there is:

Dry All Night: The Picture Book Technique That Stops Bed-wetting by Alison Mack *(Little Brown)*. There is an illustrated story for children encouraging self-charting, bladder exercises and creative visualization.

Sammy the Elephant & Mr. Camel: A Story to Help Children Overcome Enuresis by Mills and Crowley *(Magination Press)*.

Dry Days Wet Nights by M. Boelts *(Albert Whitman, 1996)*.

Accidental Lily by Sally Warner *(Knopf, 2000)*.

Do Little Mermaids Wet Their Beds? by Jeanne Willis *(Albert Whitman, 2001)*.

For my eight-year-old who goes on sleepovers, we put a plastic sheet and a beach towel in the bottom of the sleeping bag which he fixes once he's there. Clean clothes are kept under his pillow. If he has wet, he gets dressed, and rolls it all up. The sleeping bag and all are washed when he gets home. He has not been embarrassed and had a great time he might have missed.

Chris Young, Fallbrook, CA

The Battle of the Bedsheets

You can't make a child stop wetting the bed at night. Only the child can do it, and then only when the brain and bladder are willing.

Many parents believe that a bed-wetter can and should be responsible for changing a wet bed and, perhaps, for laundering the sheets. They do this not to embarrass or punish the child, but for practical reasons. It is one way to teach a child that people are expected to clean up after themselves. For some it's been all the motivation they need but not for all. At any rate, the process of cleaning up—or keeping bedding dry—should be made as painless (for you *and* your child) and as efficient as possible.

- Make up a bed with two sets of bedding (including two rubber sheets) so only the top set needs to be stripped during the night. If fitted sheets are too hard for your child to manage, use flat sheets instead.

- Use an old waterproof crib sheet, plastic tablecloth, shower curtain or a large plastic garbage bag to protect the mattress if you don't have rubber sheets or a plastic mattress cover.

- Cover your sheets with a rubberized flannel pad like the pads you used for your baby. If a juvenile bedding store doesn't have it in a large size, check out a fabric store. They often sell it by the yard.

- Buy a good protective bed sheet from a medical supply store. They are light weight. (See page 43.)

- Line the bed with a large bath towel tucked in sideways over a plastic protector. If the bed isn't too wet, the child can simply pull off the towel and go back to sleep.

- Don't forget to protect the pillow with a zippered plastic cover. Kids do move around a lot at night.

The Disposable Choice

Unfortunately bed-wetting is an inconvenience that must be dealt with. The choice boils down to doing laundry *(bedding or cloth training pants)* or using disposables *(a diaper/pant or a bed pad)*. Here are options and outlets for disposables. (See page 38 for cloth diaper information.)

In regular outlets you should be able to find:

Easy Ups™ from Pampers®.
Available in M *(22-35 lbs)*, L *(30+ lbs)* and XL *(37+ lbs)*

Pull-Ups® Training Pants from Huggies®
Disposable pull-on diapers with a stretch ability.
Available in L *(39-59 lbs)*. www.pull-ups.com

Goodnites®from Huggies®
Disposables that look and feel like white underwear.
available in M *(45-65 lbs)*, L *(65-85 lbs)* and XL *(65-85 lbs)*. www.goodnites.com.

Sleep Drys from Luvs®
Pull–up diapers available in M *(45-65 lbs)*, L *(65-85 lbs)* and XL *(85-125 lbs)*. www.sleepdrys.com

When regular disposables no longer fit:

If your child outgrows standard disposables but not the need for them, look to these resources:

Youth Briefs by Attends®
This is a small version of Attends® for children 35 lbs to 70 lbs.

Attends® **Briefs**
These side-tape disposables from Procter and Gamble come S *(20"– 31")*, M *(32"– 44")* and L *(45"– 58")* as waist/hip measurements. Found in home medical supply stores if not elsewhere.

Surety's® Fitted Briefs
Depends® Fitted or Overnight Briefs
These are two brands which are disposable, tape-tab
diapers that fit up to a 28" waist.

Tranquility®Slimline Disposable Briefs
Disposable, side-taped closing, youth underpants
start for 35 lbs/18" to 28" waist/hips.

All of these are available for home delivery from HDIS.
Call 800-538-1036 or go to their website: www.HDIS.com.

If you prefer to use disposable underpads:

Disposable bedpad liners or underpads in approximate 30"
to 36" squares can save a lot of laundry though they do not come
cheap. *Tuckables,* for instance, have side flaps that tuck under the
mattress to hold them in place. Some supermarkets and drugstores
carry some brands. You can check your hospital supply store,
these websites, or call these resources for ordering information.

Direct Medical *(www.tenadirect.com)*   800-659-8037
Paper-Pak Products *(www.paperpak.com)*   800-635-4560
Diapersite.com *(www.diapersite.com)*   888-254-8433
HDIS *(www.hdis.com))*   800-538-1036

*(HDIS offers sample assortment packs of briefs and underpads so you
can decide which items will work best for you. Call for information.)*

These are just a few of the many companies that offer
products to help you deal with bed-wetting using disposables.

- Use one-piece washable coverlets to avoid the extra top sheet getting wet and you'll have one piece less to wash.

- Keep a sleeping bag nearby for a child to finish off a night's sleep if neither of you plan to change bedding.

- Keep an extra set of pajamas available and keep a plastic laundry basket or plastic bag handy for wet bedding.

- If you haven't protected your mattress well enough, sprinkle baking soda on the wet area. It absorbs the moisture, but more importantly, the odor. Urine doesn't contain bacteria, so just drying out blankets is okay unless you need to deal with odor.

- Encourage a child who wets to shower in the morning. The telltale odor of urine needs to be avoided.

- Be sure to have a sturdy washing machine.

I use *Nikky Dry Bed* pants on my four-and-one half-year-old who wets about half the time. These cotton underpants are thickly lined and very absorbent. These pants really do keep the bed dry. They are fairly expensive but they are easier to wash than a whole set of sheets.

Martha Sherman, Falls Church, VA

My five-year-old was a very sound sleeper and never woke at night. He wore a diaper and we never made an issue of it. We tried bladder training exercises suggested by the doctor but he got frustrated. Then I bought an alarm that attached to his underpants that went off at the first sign of dampness. Within a week he was dry all night.

Peggy Robinson-Wilson, Anchorage, AK

I'd double make the bed with one waterproof pad and a sheet, and a second pad and sheet on top. At night we could just strip off the wet layer—having dry ones underneath—and put her in dry pajamas.

Lois Patterson, Bloomington, WI

I discovered that using a bath rug with rubber backing to be excellent bed protection, especially when traveling with the kids. They come in various sizes and can easily be rolled up and packed.

Cinda Elser, North Lima, OH

When my daughter was wetting her bed, I took her much loved Sesame Street sheets off. I told her they weren't going back on until she stopped wetting because Big Bird did not like to be all wet. She never wet again. (*I hope this works on my twin boys!*)

Rebecca Kerr, Chittenango, NY

Helpful Signaling Devices

In general, moisture alarms are not suggested for use until a child is 5 or 6 years old since a child needs to be cognitively involved and active in the program. The primary principle of these alarms is to awaken children while they are just starting to urinate. At first, a child probably will not wake up until the bladder is completely emptied. However, as conditioning progresses, a child begins to awaken at the first drop of wetness thus helping a child learn to wake up to the feeling of a full bladder.

The wet-sensitive alarm pad is giving way to smaller, less intrusive devices that clip on children's clothes or wrist with a wet-sensor cord that is attached to underwear. Often a bedpad alarm has to be saturated to respond, but those worn by a child are placed more strategically so they respond to the first sign of wetness, allowing a child to awaken before the bladder has completely emptied.

The disadvantages of the alarm are fairly obvious. The sound may be upsetting (*though some children have been known to sleep through it*) and disrupt other's sleep. Siblings may awaken—the last thing an embarrassed child wants to have happen. You must be willing to get up when the alarm first sounds and wake your child if it wasn't heard. Alarms have to be reset. On the plus side, alarms have a high success rate, with reports of 75% to 85% effectiveness in a week to a few months.

I had a horrible bedwetting problem as a child. It was agonizing. When I was seven or eight my mother used an alarm system which was triggered by dampness and woke me up "just in time" every night. It was terrific! For the first time in my life I learned nighttime control (in less than a week) and I felt like a normal person!

Anonymous, Minneapolis, MN

Cause for Alarm

These are some of the popular alarm devices on the market. There are alarms available through the Sears and J.C. Penny catalogs. Some medical supply companies or pharmaceutical departments will order one for you. Others are available by mail.

Wet-NO-More II
Travis International
625 H Street
Coos Bay, OR 97420
800-4-DRY BED
541-269-6900
www.wet-no-more-now.com

A comfortable sensor attaches to a foam belt or underwear for males and females. No wires. Unlimited free 800 phone counseling covering the product program. For ages 5-10 and under 100 lbs. Available by mail only for under $90. (Also available are wireless models from $185 to $250.)

SleepDry Alarm
StarChild/Labs
PO Box 404
Aptos, CA 95001
800-346-7283
831-662-2659

This system is available through pharmacies, doctors and bed-wetting clinics but can also be ordered direct for children 5 years or older. They offer a complete satisfaction guarantee as well as phone counseling. The product is the size of a small match box. It snaps on to clothes and the sensor is also non-instrusive. Under $60.

Wet-Stop
Palco Labs
8030 Soquel Ave
Santa Cruz, CA 95062
800-346-4488
831-476-3151
www.wet-stop.com

The Wet-Stop is similarly small in size to the SleepDry Alarm but differs in attachment systems. The essential difference is a soft cotton pad for the underwear which is attached to the urine sensor with Velcro. They offer a guarantee of success within 12 months. The price is under $100.

Nytone Enuretic Alarm
Nytone Medical Products
2424 South 900 West
Salt Lake City, UT 84119
801-973-4090
www.nytone.com

The small alarm attaches to the wrist with a moisture sensor that clips to the outside of underpants. Telephone consultation available. Available in pharmacies, home healthcare stores, and by mail. Suggested retail price under $65.

Potty Pager
Ideas for Living
1285 N. Cedarbrook
Boulder, CO 80304
800-497-6573
303-440-8517
www.pottypager.com

This small alarm that is inserted in underpants (no wires) does not buzz but vibrates in an on/off cycle to awaken a child after moisture activates it. Under $70.

Several companies offer conditioning devices for bed-wetters with counseling. The fees are not low but they work with you and don't leave you alone with alarm devices because they feel that support and proper use is the key to success.

ERD *(Enuresis Research & Development Center)*
PO Box 2114
Oceanside, CA 92054
888-423-3938
www.stopbedwettingfree.com

This service offers one-on-one counseling that is individually designed with a behavior modification program that includes an alarm. There are programs at three price points that range from $100 to $995. Their service claims a success rate of more than 90%.

Pacific International
555 Birch Street
Nekoosa, WI 54457
800-447-2233
715-886-4550
www.stopwetting.com

This company has been around many years and advertises widely. The alarm system they loan you, is made by them and contracted with you through a consultant. When finished, the system must be returned. If used with a second child, the cost is 50% of the original fee. The cost is not low and prices are not given, for the most part, over the phone.

Drug Therapy for Helping the Bed-wetter

Drug therapy can be effective but should be reserved for children past the age of six and be discussed, prescribed and monitored by your child's pediatric heath care provider. It seems to work for some children but not for others. Drugs offer quick results, but once stopped, a large percentage of children return to bed-wetting. Some parents and professionals discourage the use of these measures, especially if they are chosen just because they're easy.

Imipramine (*aka* Tofranil, SK-Pramine, Janimine, or Imavate), has been commonly used to treat bedwetting for many years but it is not recommended by the American Academy of Pediatrics. It is a toxic drug and antidepressant that can cause personality changes and lethargy. If used, it must be closely monitored.

Another drug you may have heard mentioned is oxybutinin (*aka* Ditropan) which is really not used for bed-wetting but only for those with proven bladder instability as reflected in daytime incontinence. It might be used with adults, not children.

The current popular prescription drug (popular in large part to the advertising campaign by the drug company, Rhône-Poulenc Roper) recently approved for enuresis treatment is desmopressin acetate (*aka* DDAVP), a synthetic version of the antidiuretic hormone, ADH. This suppresses the kidneys from making urine which some question as a viable therapy by creating this temporary, artificial response. It comes as a nasal spray and with a VERY high price tag. It is not to be used by those with cystic fibrosis, nasal polyps, epilepsy, heart or kidney disease. Some doctors like to use it because of its fast effect for success; others like it for the short term to get a jump start on successes when used in conjunction with other methods. Relapse rates after use is discontinued is high.

- Remember that any drug can be lethal in the wrong hands. If you are using a drug to treat your child's bed- wetting, be sure it is stored safely out of the child's reach, and away from siblings too. Children have died from overdoses of these drugs.

• Drugs and alarm devices are sometimes used together to treat enuresis. Again, ask your doctor (or some other professional) and use common sense to help you decide what's best for your child.

• Try to keep the problem in perspective. You and your child should decide together—with advice from caring professionals—what is best for your situation.

National Enuresis Society

This association was formed in 1992 to disseminate information to parents and professionals advising them of methods to help children overcome this problem rather than just waiting until it is outgrown. It is now part of the National Kidney Foundation. For information, contact:

NES, 1-800-WAKE-DRY, www.bedwetting-NKFonline.org

A Mayo Clinic study compared different treatment alternatives, reported in *Pediatric Primary Care* (November 1994). The drug therapies included Tofranil, DDAVP, bed-wetting alarms and time. The real success of any treatment was measured by whether the child remained dry at night after the treatment was stopped. Six months after the treatment was stopped, only 14% of the children treated with Tofranil were still dry, only 11% of the DDAVP group were, and 53% of the group using the alarm were dry at night. For the control group (children not treated but left only to time) 15% were also dry. Even in recent years, these results still hold true.

One Last Therapy

While I admit my bias prevents me from encouraging this last therapy, I would be wrong not to mention it for those who wish to pursue this route. Many chiropractors treat bed-wetting through spinal adjustments and many families have found (according to a *Dear Abby* column) success at their hands. But there is nothing that even chiropractors can point to in their own literature with controlled studies giving statistical validity (*and studies have been done*) to this premise despite testimonial evidence of success.

INDEX

Books by Vicki Lansky

- Feed Me I'm Yours
- Taming of the C.A.N.D.Y. Monster cookbook
- Games Babies Play: Birth to 12 Months
- Practical Parenting Tips Years 1–5
- Toilet Training *with* KoKo's New Potty
- KoKo Bear's New Potty
- Birthday Parties for ages 1-8
- Welcoming Your Second Baby
- A New Baby at KoKo Bear's House
- KoKo Bear's Big Earache
- Getting Your Child to Sleep...and Back to Sleep
- Trouble-Free Travel

with Children • Baby Proofing Basics • Dear Babysitter Handbook • Divorce Book for Parents • It's Not Your Fault, KoKo Bear • 101 Ways to Tell Your Child *I Love You* • 101 Ways to Make Your Child Feel Special • 101 Ways to Say *I Love You (for adults)* • 101 Ways to be a Special Dad • Kids Cooking • Best New Baby Tips • A Letter to My Baby *and several household help books, such as* Baking Soda: Over 500 Fabulous Fun and Frugal Uses *and* Another Use For...101 Common Household Items.

For a free mail order catalog listing all Lansky's books or to charge an order, call **1-800-255-3379**, or write to:

PRACTICAL PARENTING, 15245 MTKA BLVD, MINNETONKA, MN 55345

www.practicalparenting.com   dearvicki@aol.com

_____ **Potty Progress Chart**

(your child's name)

Sunday

Monday

Tuesday

Wednesday

Thursday

Friday

Saturday

Use this chart by the day of the week or just consecutive "success" days. Fill in the box with a check, star or sticker for each appropriate use of the potty seat or toilet. After 5-7 "success" days (some accidents are normal), fill-in and post the Potty Diploma. *Additional copies of this chart can be printed out at www.practicalparenting.com/pottyprogresschart.html, or enlarge this one on a photocopy machine.*

Seal of Success

Potty Diploma

This certifies that

_____

has successfully completed
the basics of grown-up
bathroom behavior as of

_____

This POTTY DIPLOMA is also on our website: www.practicalparenting.com/pottydiploma.html. You can print out a copy in color from there

_____
(your child's name)

Potty Progress Chart

Sunday ☐ ☐ ☐ ☐

Monday ☐ ☐ ☐ ☐

Tuesday ☐ ☐ ☐ ☐

Wednesday ☐ ☐ ☐ ☐

Thursday ☐ ☐ ☐ ☐

Friday ☐ ☐ ☐ ☐

Saturday ☐ ☐ ☐ ☐

Use this chart by the day of the week or just consecutive "success" days. Fill in the box with a check, star or sticker for each appropriate use of the potty seat or toilet. After 5-7 "success" days (some accidents are normal), fill-in and post the Potty Diploma. Additional copies of this chart can be printed out at www.practicalparenting.com/pottyprogresschart.html, or enlarge this one on a photocopy machine.

**Seal
of
Success**

Potty Diploma

This certifies that

_____

has successfully completed
the basics of grown-up
bathroom behavior as of

_____